Al Pacino

Biography

Sonny Boy's Journey Through Hollywood

CONTENT

Chapter 1. A Blade of Grass

Chapter 2. A Change

Chapter 3. A Tiger and an Indian

Chapter 4. The New World

Chapter 5. Grown-ups Don't Do Things Like This

Chapter 6. The Business We've Chosen

Chapter 7. Maximum Velocity

Chapter 8. Every Day Above Ground Is a Good Day

Chapter 9. It's Over

Chapter 10. Just When I Thought I Was Out

Chapter 11. Forty Dollars a Day (and All the Donuts You Can Eat)

Chapter 12. You Can Always Buy New Friends

Chapter 13. The Undiscovered Country

Chapter 14. Who Speaks of Triumph? To Endure Is Everything

Chapter 1: A Blade of Grass

I've been performing since I was a tiny lad. My mother would take me to the movies when I was three or four. She worked menial and factory jobs during the day, and when she got home, she was alone with her son. So she'd take me with her to the movies. She didn't know she was offering me a future. I was initially drawn to seeing actors on film. Because I never had playmates in our apartment and we didn't have television, I would have nothing but time to reflect about the last movie I saw. I'd run through the characters in my thoughts, bringing them to life one by one in the apartment. I learned from a young age to befriend my imagination. Being content in your solitude can be a mixed gift, especially for others with whom you spend your life.

My father was eighteen when I was born, and my mother was only a few years older. Simply put, they were youthful for their time. I was probably not even two when they divorced. My mother and I spent the first few years of our lives continuously traveling about, with little sense of stability or assurance. We shared furnished rooms in Harlem before moving into her parents' apartment in the South Bronx. My father gave us little support. A court eventually awarded us five dollars per month, which was sufficient to fund our room and board at her parents' house.

Later in life, while I was performing in my first Broadway production, relatives from my father's side of the family came to watch me. I was a young, avant-garde actor who had spent the majority of his career in Greenwich Village before making his way to Broadway. Following the play, a couple of my aunts and one or two of their children paid me a surprise visit in the backstage hallway. They started kissing, hugging, congratulating me. They were Pacinos, and although knowing them from periodic visits to my grandma on my father's side, I felt embarrassed.

My father's mother was Josephine, and she was one of the most wonderful people I've ever known. She was a deity. She just had this heavenly expression. She was the type of woman who, in the past, would travel to Ellis Island and wait for new arrivals, Italians and anyone else who didn't speak English, so she could assist them. She cared and fought for me so much that she was granted visiting rights in my parents' divorce settlement. Her husband, Alfred Pacino, my grandfather and namesake, arrived in New York from Italy in the early twentieth century. They had an arranged marriage, and my grandfather worked as a house painter. He drank heavily, which made him cranky and unpredictable.

I have no recollection of the time I spent at their home away from my mother. I suppose my mother felt bad about the arrangement. She must have. Sure, I wasn't separated from my mother for very long, but eight months was plenty of time at that age. When my son Anton was a tiny boy, not yet two years old, and I recall a moment when we were together on Seventy-Ninth Street and Broadway and his mother was not around. He had a look on his face like he was totally lost. I reasoned that it was because he was unaware of his mother's location. He was actively seeking for her, peering beyond other people on the street to see if he could spot her. He was the same age I was when I lived with my father's parents. I've never seen my son so lost at sea, before or since.

My mother's parents resided in a six-story tenement on Bryant Avenue in the South Bronx, in a top-floor apartment with the lowest rents. It was a swarm of perpetual activity, with only three rooms, all serving as bedrooms. These were small rooms, but they did not seem small to me. We could sometimes have up to six or seven people living there at once. We lived in shifts. Nobody had their own room, so I spent a lot of time sleeping between my grandparents. Other times, when I slept on a daybed in what was intended to be the living room, I had no idea who would wind up camped out next to me—a relative traveling through town or my mother's brother, returning from his own service in the war. He had served in the Pacific, and like many other combat veterans, he refused to discuss his wartime experiences. He would put wooden matchsticks in his ears to block off the explosions he couldn't stop hearing.

My mother's father's name was Vincenzo Giovanni Gerardi, and he came from an old Sicilian town called Corleone. When he was four, he immigrated to America, possibly illegally, and took the name James Gerard. By then, he had already lost his mother; his father, who was somewhat of a dictator, had remarried and relocated to Harlem with his children and new wife. My grandfather had a chaotic, Dickensian upbringing, yet he was the first true father figure I had.

Our tenement housed families from all across Eastern Europe and the rest of the world. You overheard a cacophony of tongues. You heard everyone. Our short area of Longfellow Avenue and Bryant Avenue, from 171st to 174th Street, was a mix of nations and cultures. In the summer, when we walked up to our tenement's roof to cool down because there was no air conditioning, we could hear numerous languages spoken in a variety of accents. It was a great time: many impoverished people from various ghettos had moved in, and we were transforming the Bronx. The families were more rich as you moved north. We were not prosperous. We were getting by. My grandfather was a plasterer and had to work daily. Plasterers were extremely popular back then. He had gained skill and was valued for what he performed. He built an alleyway wall for our landlord, who was so pleased with the wall that he kept our family's rent at $38.80 per month for the duration of our lease.

I wasn't permitted to leave the tenement alone until I was a little older—we lived in the back, and the neighborhood was quite unsafe—and I didn't have any siblings. We didn't have a television or much entertainment, other than a couple of Al Jolson albums that I used to mime to for my family when I was three or four. My only companions, aside from my grandparents, mother, and a tiny puppy named Trixie, were the characters I created from the movies my mother took me to. I had to be the sole five-year-old who was taken to The Lost Weekend. I was particularly impressed with Ray Milland's Oscar-winning performance as a self-destructive alcoholic. When he is trying to get dry and suffering from the d.t. he has a vision of a bat swooping from a corner of his hospital room and attacking a mouse climbing the wall. Milland might convince you he's trapped in this fantasy horror. I can't forget the moment where he's sober and desperately looking for the booze he stashed away when he was drunk but can't remember where he hid it. I'd try to do it myself, pretending to raid a phantom apartment while I rummaged through unseen cabinets, drawers, and hampers. I became so adept at this little performance that I would perform it on request for my relatives. They'd roar with laughter. I suppose it struck them as amusing to witness a five-year-old pretending to scramble through an imaginary kitchen with life-or-death urgency. That was an energy within myself that I was already realizing I could harness.

My mother had a sensitivity to these issues. I believe it is why she was drawn to these types of flicks. She was a stunning woman, yet she was delicate and had fragile feelings. She would occasionally visit a psychiatrist when Granddad had the funds to pay for her appointments. I had no idea my mother was having troubles until one day when I was six. I was getting ready to go out and play in the streets, sitting in a chair in the kitchen as my mother laced up my small shoes and wrapped a sweater around me to keep me warm. I noticed she was crying and wondered what was wrong, but I wasn't sure how to question her. She was kissing me all over, and she gave me a big embrace as I left the apartment. It was weird, but I was eager to get downstairs and meet the other kids, so I gave it little further consideration.

As a child, my interactions with my street friends gave me strength and optimism. I ran with my three best buddies, Cliffy, Bruce, and Petey. Each day was a new adventure. We were on the hunt, eager for life. In retrospect, I believe I might have received more love from my family than the other three. I believe that may have made all the difference. I survived, but they didn't.

One of my favorite recollections is walking down the stairs and out onto the street in front of my tenement building on a Saturday morning in the spring. I couldn't have been older than ten years. The street was vacant, and the day was bright. I recall glancing down the block and seeing Bruce about 50 yards away. I felt this euphoria inside of me that has stayed with me forever. The day was clear and crisp, and everything was calm and motionless. He turned and grinned, and so did I, since we both knew we were still alive. The day was full of opportunities. Something was about to happen.

Often, I'd be playing baseball in one of those lots when I noticed Granddad in the distance, going by on his way home from work. No matter where I was in the lot, as soon as I caught sight of him, I'd dash over to meet him on the sidewalk just as he passed by, shaking him down for enough stray change to get an ice cream. If I saw him walking by while I was at bat, I'd cry out to grab his attention, hoping he'd see me crack the ball and reach base. He'd pause and watch for a minute, and every time he stood there, I'd strike out. Every single time. When I returned home, I told him that after he left, I received a triple, and he nodded and smiled.

In the neighborhood, I appeared to defy death on a regular basis. I was like a cat with far more than nine lives. I've experienced more blunders and accidents than I can count, so I'll choose a couple that stand out and have meaning. One winter day, I was skating on the ice above the Bronx River. We didn't have ice skates, so I was doing pirouettes in sneakers in front of my friend Jesus Diaz, who was standing on the shore. I was laughing, and he was cheering me on, when I abruptly broke through the surface and crashed into the frigid waters below. Every time I tried to crawl out, the ice broke and I fell back into the frigid water. I believe I would have drowned that day if not for Jesus Diaz. He found a large stick twice his size, spread himself out as far as he could from the shore, and used it to pull me to safety. I was soaked and freezing, so he took me out of the cold and into the flat he lived with his family in the tenement where his father worked as the supervisor. Jesus Diaz offered me his clothes.

Our South Bronx neighborhood was full of crazy individuals, most of whom were innocent. We saw a man in his late thirties or early forties dressed in a suit and a collared shirt with a loose, frayed tie. His hair was a mix of red and black. He appeared to have attended a Sunday church and been covered with ashes. Sure, like everyone, I was wary of him. We were like a pack of wild animals, and we recognized he was different from our kind. Our instincts told us he was separate, so we didn't ask. We just accepted him. People treated each other with more decency and distance than they do now. Perhaps it still exists in smaller communities, and that is something I have always carried with me through life.

Steve had no idea what was going on, and neither did I, given my youth. I lacked the nuance and experience. Later in life, I would comprehend what I believe may have happened to him. It was something that might happen on any street in any town, and it had happened right here. In my mind, I found a method to get past it. There are things that happen to us as we grow up, and while they hit us, we can't completely compute or recall anything about them unless we are put into a hypnotic state. But we absorb them anyway. I understood right away that something had gone horribly wrong, and Steve appeared to be broken and powerless as a result.

All I knew was that with pals like Cliffy, Bruce, and Petey, I would never feel powerless. When we were a bit older, about eleven or twelve, we formed gangs and explored the area, venturing beyond the end of our block in search of new opportunities. You went to one place and the gang beat you. You traveled to another spot and were attacked by another gang. You quickly learnt the boundaries of your own land and did your best to stay put.

We did whatever fun we could afford to do. We spent hours lying flat on our bellies fishing in the sewer gratings at the extremities of our blocks, hoping to see something shiny in the grime that could be a misplaced coin. This was not an idle effort. Fifty cents was a game changer. We would climb to the tops of tenements and jump from one roof to another. On Saturday nights, when we spotted boys just a few years older than us who had advanced to dating girls and were taking their dates to the movies or the metro, we'd jump up on the storefront rooftops and throw rubbish at them. Sometimes we'd cut up a head of lettuce and throw it at them. A string bean hurled from twenty feet away has the potential to sting. We opened hydrants during the summer, making us heroes to all the young mothers who let their small children play in the water. In mid-July, temperatures in the South Bronx would rise significantly. We hitched to the back of buses and leaped over subway turnstiles. If we desired food, we would steal it. We've never paid for anything.

In addition to me, Bruce, Petey, and Cliffy, my little crew included Jesus Diaz, Bibby, Johnny Rivera, Smoky, Salty, and Kenny Lipper, who would one day become a deputy mayor of New York City under Ed Koch. (I later appeared in City Hall, a film directed by Harold Becker and based on his experience, in which I co-starred with John Cusack.)

We also had a child named Hymie in our group who nowadays would be classified as special needs. He was older than us and much stronger. Other gangs would think twice if they saw him. That was an old World War II ballad about a soldier missing his girl at home. When Hymie turned sixteen, he got violent, attacking his mother, and he was placed in an institution. We never saw him again. We

9

missed him.

Cliffy, Bruce, Petey and I were the top four bananas. They called me Sonny and Pacchi, Pacino's nickname. They also dubbed me Pistachio because I enjoyed pistachio ice cream. If we had to choose a leader, it would be Cliffy or Petey. Petey was a tough Irish youngster. But Cliffy was a prodigy, a true original, courageous, and never left home without a copy of Dostoevsky in his back pocket, even at the age of thirteen. This boy had the capacity to become whatever he desired in life. He had talent. He had the look. He had a very high IQ, which he used to gloat about. And he had four older brothers who beat the crap out of him every day. He was full of tricks. You never had to ask him, "What are we doing today?" He always had a plan.

We would walk up to the rooftops of the tenements to hang out, and they also served as escape routes if we were being pursued. TV antennas were erected along a twelve-inch ledge that ran around the building's perimeter. We used to walk along that ledge as if we were in a high-wire act. We'd move like cats five floors high, and when we reached one of those antennas, we'd pause to calm ourselves before continuing on. We'd travel over by the Bronx Zoo to what they used to call Monkey Island, where we'd climb up the big ropes strung around tree branches by some distant ancestor of ours. We'd swing on those ropes out over the pond, let go, and play in the water. Bruce emerged from there with a leech attached to his body, draining blood. Some of the guys who were older than us would stand on a large, flat rock that extended into the sea and compete to see who could jerk off the furthest.

Cliffy once observed a squirrel scamper up a tree and tossed a rock at it. Cliffy burst into tears as the poor squirrel died on the ground with a thump. He didn't believe he'd kill it. We buried the squirrel and prayed over it. Another time, I came home with an injured sparrow that I had found and brought to my mother, and we took good care of it. After a while, this sparrow became accustomed to us. It would fly about the apartment, landing on our shoulders. We just had to make sure the dog stayed away from it. We all really liked it. My mother used to kiss it, and we made it a small birdcage. She fed it to restore its vigor, and she cared for, petted, and loved it. We finally had to let it go because we felt it needed to be free. We brought it back to where the other sparrows were and released it. It was smaller than the other sparrows, and we later learned that they normally rejected tamed birds. We were heartbroken to learn that our friend had most likely been killed by his own kind due to our friendship.

My grandmother cleaned our kitchen window the same way most tenement inhabitants do: she opened it, sat on the windowsill, and washed the window from the outside, while her backside dangled precariously out of the window frame five floors above earth. When I stood in the kitchen and looked out that window, I could see down into the alleyway where my grandfather had built the wall that separated our alleyway from the alleyway of the next-door building. If you went over that wall, you would find a tunnel that led to a vast network of exits and entrances, a universe unto itself, with passages connecting courtyards and circular spaces. When I first started smoking cigarettes between the ages of ten and eleven, I made sure I was in an alleyway where no one could see me, because I knew smoking was prohibited. I believe shady things were done down there, whatever was illegal. It had that sense, yet it was not frightening; rather, it was inviting. The first time I kissed a female was in those lanes. I had no idea what I was doing, but I assumed something wonderful had occurred. I thought I had lost my virginity. Unfortunately not.

Sports were an area that set me apart from the rest of the gang. My grandfather fostered a passion for sports in me. He was a longtime baseball and boxing fan. He grew up rooting for the New York Yankees before they were even called the Yankees—they were formerly known as the Highlanders—and as a poor boy, he would watch their games through gaps in the fence at Hilltop Park or the Polo Grounds, where the New York Giants played. Later, the Yankees would have their own stadium, known as the House That Ruth Built. That stadium appears in the background of a sequence in Serpico, which Sidney Lumet photographed with such perfection, in which Serpico meets with the corrupt officers who have gathered like a nest of thieves. The scene was shot Tuesday morning. Weld and I split up, and you can tell by the look on my face that he's devastated.

My grandfather was always a supporter of the underdog, and it appears that I am as well. I always pull for the losers until they start winning, at which point I remark to myself, "Oh man, I'm no longer rooting for them."

When he could afford it, Granddad would take me to baseball games and sit far up in the grandstand—the cheap seats. Of course, we were aware that there were box tickets available at a higher price and closer to the field. this was another matter entirely—we did not belong in the class. I didn't consider myself to be disadvantaged; it was simply another block in the neighborhood, another clan. It could have been another nation. Cliffy and I differed in that Cliffy saw the identical box seats and wanted to go down there. If there was a line to get into a movie, he would cut in front of someone and walk right in. He was courageous in that regard. It was as if no one lived but him. He was a solipsist if I ever saw one. When I think about it, I might be somewhere along that spectrum too.

I was an athlete at that age. I was quick and nimble, and I bounced around as I moved. I played baseball for my neighborhood's PAL team. Cliffy and the guys had no interest in sports, so it was almost as if I lived two lives: one with the group and another with the people I played ball with. For a while, I imagined I'd grow up to be a professional baseball player, until I saw some of those people play for the Yankees' farm team—they couldn't even be looked at, yet they were far better than me, to be honest. I am in awe of elite athletes. You have to climb a mountain to get there, and they've all summited Mount Everest, as far as I know.

You'd occasionally hear a muffled gunshot, usually from a handmade gun constructed of wood and elastic bands. It was similar to a slingshot in that if you added a.22-caliber bullet and ignited the shell, it would normally go sideways; if you were unfortunate, it would fly up toward your head. You shot them at cans, bottles, and rocks, but they had an impact. If you carried one, it provided you the extra step you needed, but it may land you in trouble. The entire area was fraught with danger, but it added to the excitement.

One day, I was on Bryant Avenue and noticed the rest of the gang limping back from the Dutchies, defeated. Cliffy was covered with blood. Petey stood behind him, his blood spilling like a volcano from a gash on his wrist. He called out a well-known name in the region. Even now, I cannot bring myself to utter it. Cliffy had merely been teasing, but the other kids scattered in all directions. Petey knew he needed to move swiftly, but he stumbled and fell, landing hard. He landed on something sharp and jagged, cutting through his left wrist. The wound was so deep that it penetrated all the way to the nerves. It was dreadful. The physicians were eventually able to heal him, but they stitched him up incorrectly, preventing him from moving properly. I believe that if it happened today, that type of injury could be properly treated—it might cost you, but it would be done well. But there he was, with a hand that he could no longer move. The dark realm of poverty had rendered him disabled. When Petey played ball with us, he had to remove his glove from the hand he had just caught the ball with and use it to throw it back. Cliffy always hated himself for Petey's misfortune, which was all the result of his idiotic prank.

But something else is preventing me from springing out of the tub, putting on my clothes, and rejoining them. I don't mean my conscience, but my mother. She tells me I'm not authorized. She says it's late, tomorrow is a school day, and any males who come to shout out in the alley at that time of night aren't the type of boys I should be hanging out with, so the answer is no.

I resent her for this. She is isolating me from the outside world. These friends form the foundation of my identity. They are everything in my life that is important to me right now, and my mother will not let me be with them. I despise her for it. And then one day I'm fifty-two, looking in the vanity mirror at my fat, shaving cream-covered face, trying to think of someone to thank in an acceptance speech for an award I'm about to get. When I reflect on that moment, I realize my mom is the reason I am still alive. Of course, it is who I must thank, yet I have never thanked her for it. She's the one who kept a lid on everything, who steered me away from the route that led to delinquency, danger, and violence, to the needle, that lethal delight known as heroin, which killed three of my best friends. Petey, Cliffy, and Bruce all perished from drugs. I wasn't precisely under severe surveillance, but my mother was more aware of my whereabouts than my friends' families were, and we all knew it. I think she saved my life.

I could tell my mother's family did not have a positive opinion of my father, but my grandparents were careful not to say anything derogatory about him in my presence. My mother, on the other hand, occasionally said things that made it plain she didn't respect him or believe he cared for me. Such rhetoric can harm young people. When you come from a broken household, you already feel like an orphan. That adult's point of view can lead to long-term prejudice—it can poison the well indefinitely—and we must exercise extreme caution. And I'm sure hearing it from her made an impact on me. Even at that age, I was determined not to let her impact my thoughts toward my father. I wanted to create his portrait.

When I was nine, my father showed me around East Harlem, where he lived. He and my mother had been divorced for a few years, and since returning from the war, he had established a new life for himself. He was in his late twenties and had received his undergraduate education through the GI Bill. From my understanding, he worked as an accountant and was doing rather well for himself. I'd see him on holidays and birthdays, and he'd moved into a new apartment, married, and had a child. He still wanted me in his life. So he drove me about his neighborhood, stopping at businesses and local hangouts to show me off to his buddies. But I had no idea who these people were. They were from a different breed. They were Italians, and they appeared to be relatives I had met, yet they spoke in a way I was unfamiliar with. They were older and drank anisette out of little espresso cups in storefront cafés. They were cool and liked me, but all I wanted to do was go home to the Bronx and spend time with my own pals. I felt like my father was putting me on display.

I've had friends throughout my childhood who liked their fathers or had close relationships with both of their parents. However, others did not have positive relationships with their fathers. Some grew up witnessing their drunken fathers beat the crap out of their mothers. I've even known folks who were so angry at their father that they became physically ill just being around him. I've just never had a father. He was absent. I consider myself very fortunate to have had my grandfather. But now that I think about it, my father's inability to develop a relationship with me must have been really terrible. He was Italian, and I was his first and only kid, so I'm sure it plagued him. At the same time, I realized I was relieved not to have that guy around. If that guy had raised me, I would not be who I am now. But I met three of his half sisters, his children, and they all spoke well of him. I could tell how much they loved him.

I had other individuals in my life who were watching out for and guiding me, even if I didn't recognize it at the time. My junior high teacher, Blanche Rothstein, a beautiful middle-aged woman, chose me to begin reading Bible passages during our student assemblies. I did not come from a highly religious family. My mother sent me to catechism class, and I wore my small white suit to my First Holy Communion. But I was afraid that if I was so good, the Virgin Mary might come down and declare me a saint. I answered no; I don't want to be a saint. That worried me, and that's the truth, so I never went back for my confirmation. That, and the nuns beat you without justification.

Soon, I was performing in school productions such as The Melting Pot, a small pageant honoring the numerous cultures whose citizens contributed to America's grandeur. I was among the children chosen to stand in front of a massive melting pot in the center of the stage. I was there representing Italy, together with a ten-year-old girl with dark hair and olive skin. I portrayed Louis, Anna's son, in our class production of The King and I. Another child who played the little Prince of Siam and I performed a song together about how we were perplexed by how adults behaved.

At the end of the year, our junior high class held an assembly to vote on several student awards, and I was chosen as Most Likely to Succeed. I was disappointed since I wanted to be the prettiest. But Willy Rams won it—he was one of those men that would do one-armed push-ups and stroll around on his hands. He was a wonderful child. But Most Likely to Succeed, which they offered me, was simply a popularity contest. All it meant was that many people had heard of you.

Blanche Rothstein, my junior high school teacher, had a grander plan for me. She climbed the five flights of stairs in our tenement to get to our apartment because she wanted to talk with my grandmother. She wasn't there to punish me, but to encourage me. My grandma didn't understand what this teacher was doing, but my mother knew, and she was concerned. As she saw it, we were poor, and poor people don't act. This had no negative impact on my academic performance. When I was thirteen, I was cast in our class play, Home Sweet Homicide, as one of the children who assist their widowed mother in solving a murder at the house next door. Before I walked on stage, someone informed me that both my parents were in the audience. My mother and father are in the audience. Oh no. It threw me off, and I did not perform as well as I had intended. To this day, I don't want to know who was in the audience on opening night or any other night.

Aside from that, performing the play was fantastic. I always felt comfortable on stage. I felt like this was where I belonged. I mean, I enjoyed being on a baseball field, but I couldn't play as well as I could in theater. I simply enjoyed it. I felt free. I felt happy. I felt people were paying attention to me. And I enjoyed interacting with the other actors. After the show, my mother and father accompanied me to Howard Johnson's, where we all celebrated my achievement. Howard Johnson's was only a diner, similar to Denny's, as shown in the beginning of Pulp Fiction. It's not fancy. Simple people go there. You do not receive a large fat cheque at the end of the meal. But I got a strong sense of warmth and belonging. It was perhaps the first time I'd ever seen my parents sitting next to each other. Can you imagine that? I had been longing for this for a long time, but I didn't realize it. Every child grows up longing to be with their mother and father. That is security. That is family.

I was discovering something I'd been missing: a sense of connectedness. I could tell they were talking to each other well, not arguing over anything. My father once caressed my mother's hand with his own; was he flirting with her? It was so natural and easy that I questioned why they ever separated. The play had brought them together, however briefly. Whatever had been weighing over me was lifted, because these two individuals would look after me right now. Acting in this play reunited my mother and father and helped me feel like I belonged again. I was genuinely whole. I had that sensation for the first time in my life. And suddenly it was gone.

Chapter 2: A Change

For many years, I used to watch movies at the old Elsmere Theatre on Crotona Parkway in the Bronx. They dubbed these structures movie palaces for a reason: they were opulent beyond belief. Sculpted faces sprung out of the walls, and chandeliers dangled high above your head. The draperies and rugs were gleaming in red and gold. Just setting foot inside such a venue for a few hours was enough to transport you away from your mundane daily life. And then, when I was fifteen years old, I noticed something I had never seen before. A company of actors appeared, as if from another century, to perform Anton Chekhov's The Seagull. The theater had a seating capacity of about two thousand people, and the play drew an audience of approximately fifteen people, maybe twenty if I am charitable. But two of those viewers were my friend Bruce and myself.

I thought it was fantastic. I didn't have anything else to compare it to at that age. It hit me like a lightning bolt from the clear blue sky. I'm not sure how much of it I actually comprehended, with all of its unrequited love and the sad figure of Konstantin, who is so frustrated in art and love, so dissatisfied with the fame that his work brings him, that he sees no other option except death. But I was captivated by the performances. Previously, I assumed poets were folks with floor-length beards. Now here I was, seeing a Russian play that may have appeared exotic to me, but I felt its power—the sense of being taken into a world I was unfamiliar with and finding myself in the lives of these fictional characters.

I had never considered what I wanted to be—I had never set a goal. Things either stuck to me or didn't. And that stuck with me. I overheard something. I began reading Chekhov for myself, bringing his volumes around with me, amazed by the prospect of having his work available anytime I wanted it. Chekhov became a buddy to me.

Cliffy and I had just passed our auditions to attend the High School of Performing Arts in Manhattan. In the mornings, we would take the train from the Bronx to Forty-Second Street and Broadway. For the four blocks we walked up to PA on Forty-Sixth Street, we were mesmerized by all the people, tourists, gawkers, and gadabouts, trying to get where they were going, while movie marquees blared their latest offerings and a sophisticated man on a billboard blew smoke rings from his Camel cigarette onto all of us. One day, as we rounded a corner, I noticed Paul Newman, the movie star, walk past us and thought, Wow, he's a real person. When there are no cameras around, he goes for walks and talks with his buddies. Cliffy missed him completely. His thoughts were elsewhere.

The class began as usual that morning, with the teacher instructing us in her deep, thunderous voice. Cliffy soon got up before her. He mentioned something to her that sparked an argument between them. The teacher began following Cliffy around the room, haplessly swinging her fists at him without success. I'll never know what he said to elicit this reaction, but I couldn't believe it was occurring right in front of us, especially because he had told me he would do it. They clenched together like wrestlers, and as they tussled, Cliffy wrapped his arms around her from behind, swung her around to face the class, and there he was, behind her, with both hands on her breasts. He looked at me and grinned.

This was an act committed by someone who had no regard for propriety, limitations, or conscience. It was so bizarre and sinister. Where did that come from? Was he reading Dostoevsky? Most of the kids remained silent. I laughed, as did another classmate, John Wilson. I am not sure why we laughed. It was simply a natural, involuntary reaction to a stunning sight. I adored Cliffy, and I was outraged by this intrusion. The disrespect for our dear instructor was horrible. Our astonished laughter was enough to get me and John kicked out of the classroom for the day, and I spent it in the principal's office until my mother came down and apologized on my behalf. Cliffy took a considerably harsher hit. He was kicked out of school, and subsequently thrown out of his house. After that, he seemed to vanish from my life for a while, though I would periodically hear about him around the neighborhood through snippets of stories about the antisocial life he was now leading.

On another day, at my meal break from Performing Arts, I went out for lunch with the money my mother had given me. I stopped into a Howard Johnson's around the corner on West Forty-Sixth Street, and behind the counter was one of the actors from The Seagull, which I had watched in the Bronx. He looked at me like, "This kid is giving me a little hope here." He was an actor I'd seen on stage, and I felt at ease speaking with him. I felt a connection with him. By day, he dressed as a waiter and served people their meals and drinks. At night, he played in a play. One was a profession that provided him with the wherewithal to keep going, and the other was his artistic passion.

This is how I began to perceive acting as a vocation. You worked while performing, and it would be ideal if you could be compensated for your efforts. He was an actor who transitioned from role to part and theater to theater, as actors have done for centuries. Actors are now widely accepted and praised in society; there are prominent acting families, and actors can even become presidents. However, it was not always a reputable occupation. Molière, the great French playwright, was shunned by his family. Theater folks are vagabonds and traveling gypsies. We are folks on the run. That, too, is our inheritance.

When I was about sixteen, my mother began dating a new suitor, the first one who appeared to be a serious partner since she and my father had separated. Their romance progressed to the point where they began to plan their wedding. I was ecstatic, and I saw she was behaving more confident than I had seen her in years. My entire life,

I've been sensitive to how others feel, and I'd notice subtle things in her—inflections in how she acted or spoke. I thought she sounded like someone else, like a teacher or a high school principal.

I was relieved, but I didn't understand how I fit into this arrangement. This man was about fifty, and she was a lovely woman with a teenage son. She was trying to indicate that this person probably does not want you around. Meanwhile, I was stuck in our apartment with her, unable to do anything. My grandparents had moved farther uptown to an apartment on 233rd Street, which they thought was a better neighborhood, so it was just me and my mother living in the old Bryant Avenue house. I figured she'd be better off with this guy. I needed her to leave there. It would set me free.

Then their engagement was unexpectedly cancelled. The guy didn't even have the decency to inform her in person that he was calling it off. He sent her a telegram saying he couldn't do it anymore. When she got the telegram, she was sitting at our kitchen table, and I was leaning against the arch of the hallway leading to it. The exit door was four feet away, and I was continually striving for it. My mom informed me the engagement was off. She was shattered. Those were terrible words. It was one of the scariest things I ever told her. I was disappointed that it was done to her in the first place, and I was concerned that she had been injured. But it disturbed me that she would not leave the house and leave it to me.

My mother did not take the breakup well. It almost devastated her. She was a Tennessee Williams character, fragile and unpredictable. Doctors diagnosed her with anxiety neurosis. She was on a downward spiral and required electroshock therapy and barbiturates. These were pricey items. My mother pushed me to quit school and go to work. We did not have the money.

I continued in school a little longer, at least until I was sixteen, when I was legally permitted to leave. Quitting school may have seemed like a tragic setback in my life, but I was fine with it. Actually, I was happy about it, which I realize is a strange attitude to have. But I've never seen school as my place. When I began to gain recognition for the wonderful work I was doing in my acting classes at school, PA chose me to represent the student body in a photo that would accompany a piece about the school in the Herald Tribune newspaper. Can you believe it? Then, at the last minute, I was removed from the story and replaced with another student studying to be a dancer. She was tall and had red hair, while I had a dark complexion and an Italian name. It occurred to me that this could be why they made the decision. She represented a more mainstream type of beauty than I did. When you looked around, you didn't see individuals like me in detergent advertisements or on soap operas. Losing this opportunity did not concern me, and I didn't think they were biased. Performing Arts was attempting to increase enrollment at the institution, which was the current situation.

So I left. I felt compelled to get out there and start working. My mom needed assistance. I have worked in various professions, all were temporary. I spent the summer working as a bicycle messenger, cycling across the city for eleven hours a day. When I was seventeen, I had a successful period working for the American Jewish Committee and their publication, Commentary. I was giving her a pitch, and I'm sure she saw right through it, yet she hired me anyhow. I'd walk into their offices first thing in the morning, prepared to leap over massive tables in a single bound. They'd send me on errands, and sometimes I wouldn't return. I had plenty of energy. It was a busy office, and I became acquainted with my coworkers. I learned how to use a switchboard and would file items for them. But at a workplace party, drink in hand, I could talk to practically anyone.

At the age of eighteen, I was drinking a fifteen-cent beer at Martin's Bar and Grill, located on Twenty-Third Street and Sixth Avenue in Manhattan. I sat there as long as I could to stay warm. The regulars who came were workers. They all seemed to be miners and lumberjacks. The bartender's name was Cookie—a huge guy with spectacles who appeared to be the opposite of Cookie, yet that's what they called him. The pub had a large picture window facing Sixth Avenue. Across from it was the Herbert Berghof Studio, an acting school I was hoping to get into. This pub occasionally served free lunch, so I'd walk in and have ketchup sandwiches, which were two saltine crackers with ketchup in the middle, and I ate my fair share of them.

I was thinking about something when Cookie suddenly became angry. He emerged from behind the bar and knocked on the door to the men's room. The next thing you know, he's grabbed two scruffy little girls by the necks of their leather jackets and is flinging them out. Something about the two girls in the restroom disturbed him. As Cookie returned to his place where all the working staff, seven or eight of them, were lined up at the bar, the two females stepped in front of that large, wide window in broad daylight and began openly, passionately, hugging and kissing each other, defying their expulsion. They were performing their actions so that everyone in the bar could see them. There was a schism I was witnessing between these two worlds: the bold girls outside, who were the epitome of liberation, and the guys at the bar, who were stunned by something they'd never seen before in their life. The Sixties were approaching, and the world was changing.

I met Charlie at the same bar later. I noticed him in a booth, wearing a baseball cap and drinking with a few others. And the instant I laid eyes on him, I thought, "This is my type of guy." He was maybe ten years older than me. When you lose your father, you are constantly looking for one in some form. When I met him, I knew. This guy is my teacher. I joined Herbert Berghof Studios. I had no money, so I cleaned the corridors and rooms where dancing classes were held, and they granted me a scholarship.

24

Charlie was knowledgeable about the world and able to draw lessons from it that I could grasp and apply to my own life. He once told me a story about the Flying Wallendas, a family of artists who would accomplish incredible tightrope walks without a net. They would sit on each other's shoulders as they crossed the high wire. The entire gang had been heaped on top of one another like a pyramid, which collapsed. Some died after falling off the high wire, while others were injured or crippled. When the remainder of the family recovered from the tragedy, they went out and repeated the act.

After class, Charlie and I would go out together. We became loyal drinking companions. His wife, Penny Allen, was also a performer, and they resided in an East Twenties apartment. They never had any money either. Charlie once came to the Commentary magazine office and asked for $5, which I gave him. Later, I lost my Commentary position. I was a man without work. My mother had gone up to 233rd Street to live with her parents, so I had our old flat to myself. I only had to pay $38.80 in rent every month. But I was broke. I had made as much money as I could by cashing in the beer bottles that were cluttering up my apartment, and now I had nothing. So I went to find Charlie, who was in Far Rockaway.

It was midsummer, and getting there from Manhattan was a journey. I took a bus to a train, then another train, switching trains at another station, and finally arriving at the end of the line. It could take hours, and all the while I was reading Balzac, Baudelaire, and Flaubert from pocket-sized books with the smallest font you've ever seen. It was a sweltering day, and when I arrived at Far Rockaway, Charlie and Penny were at the beach with their newborn girl, Deirdre. I saw them beside the surf while going on the sand dressed entirely in black—shoes, pants, shirt, leather jacket—doing my Paladin thing. Then I boarded the train and began my long and arduous journey back to Manhattan, reading my little books along the way.

Matt Clark, a friend from Charlie's acting class, oversaw our move.

He had begun with a tiny truck, transporting pieces of art in the Village, then progressed to relocating apartments and purchasing a larger vehicle to accommodate larger workplaces. He was good at both this and acting. How does an actor prepare? He carries the refrigerator up the stairs. Matt Clark looked at me like I was from the Bronx, but he let me tag around and make a little money, mostly because Charlie would vouch for me. I got on Matt's wrong side when I dropped the end of a refrigerator while walking up a five-story walk-up. Another day we were moving to an office, and as usual, I left. I ended up at some Christmas party on that floor. I was eating a meal, sipping a Scotch, and flirting with a few gals. Our work had paused for a while, and I decided I was due for a rest.

We never had a telephone in our apartment when I was growing up, but now I have one. I received a call from my father, whom I had not heard from in months. His second marriage had failed exactly like the first, and he had relocated to Los Angeles, where he was once again enjoying life as a single guy, and he invited me to join him. The poor man wanted to connect with his son, and he realized he had something to offer me. He didn't realize his son was an aspiring poet, artist, and Chekhov wannabe. I didn't care about girls—well, I did, but I didn't comprehend them or notice that they were interested in me. It took me a lifetime to realize that my father was only trying to reach out to me in the way he thought was best.

I had to pay rent while I was living alone. I attempted being a busboy but didn't make it. They found me eating leftovers from the tables. That is how hungry I was. In my spare time, I was a wanderer. I would roam the streets all day, then sit in the library for warmth. But I became an avid reader. I had no teachers and no schoolwork, so I pursued my own interests. Charlie Laughton assisted in recommending various writers, books to read, and locations to visit, such as the Forty-Second Street Library for warmth and the Automat for food. At the Automat, I could make a single cup of coffee to last all morning and sit there for five hours reading my tiny books by famous authors. There was something captivating about the talent of reading. It could relax your thoughts and give you another world to explore. Television was too far away; books felt more intimate, like spending time with friends. I'd be reading A Moveable Feast and thinking, "I don't want to finish the pages because I enjoy it here so much."

When I was approximately nineteen or twenty, Charlie and I returned to my Bronx apartment after one of our long walks and conversations. As I looked in my mailbox, he started climbing the stairs. And Charlie never spoke like that. I mean, never. He never mentioned it to me the whole time I knew him. That wasn't his deal at all. It appeared out of nowhere. Martin Sheen, another young actor in Charlie's class, was my classmate. Marty performed a monologue from The Iceman Cometh during one session, and he blew the roof off—I thought, this is it, we're watching a brilliant actor. I considered him to be the next James Dean.

Martin Sheen moved with me to the South Bronx so we could split rent. We worked together at the Living Theatre in Greenwich Village, cleaning bathrooms and laying down rugs for the sets of the plays they performed. Judith Malina and Julian Beck, two actors who were true visionaries, formed the Living Theatre in their living room in the 1950s and then relocated it to Fourteenth Street and Sixth Avenue. They did the kind of concerts that made you go home, lock yourself in your room, and cry for two days while staring at the ceiling. They had that kind of influence. They pioneered off-Broadway theatre, and its popularity paved the door for off-off-Broadway theatre. That enabled some of the off-off-off-off-Broadway productions I was creating, in which actors performed for audiences drinking coffee and eating pastries in Village cafés. When I did Hello Out There by William Saroyan, we would put on sixteen performances every week at Caffe Cino on Cornelia Street and pass the hat to the small audience, trying to get a few dollars to eat. When you played there, there was always a passing of the hat. That is how you ate and supported your habit. It was our Paris in the early 1900s, and Berlin in the 1920s. A renaissance is happening in our beautiful city, New York. Sartre, Ibsen, Bertolt Brecht, Leonard Melfi, Allen Ginsberg, Ferlinghetti, Kerouac, and Sam Shepard all contributed to the scene's spirit and vitality. We inherited the world they created.

Other folks would come and go until I finally gave up on the Bronx apartment. Marty's siblings would occasionally stay over, as would Sal Russo from acting class, who was accompanying Sandra. Her dearest friend was Joan Baez, a musician with long dark hair and piercing eyes who would periodically stop by the apartment, sit cross-legged in a corner, and play her guitar. Joan hadn't met Bob Dylan yet, but we knew she was going places. I can't believe we even exchanged hellos. She was simply one of the many people that passed through our apartment as the world revolved around us.

Cliffy was back in the neighborhood. Both he and Bruce had joined the army. Bruce made it all the way to his induction ceremony before having second thoughts, pretending to flip out, and threatening to jump out a window, so he was released. Cliffy, on the other hand, stayed long enough to serve for a few months. He ran into problems and was sent to the brig before being thrown out. I knew I wasn't at risk of being drafted because I was supporting my mother. He was aware of how odd and anxious I was. Cliffy had left the service in poor health. He was on the needle now, doing and talking strange things. He claimed to have served in the same platoon as Elvis Presley, which turned out to be true. He claimed to have traveled to Canada, gotten a Catholic girl pregnant, and converted from Judaism so that they might marry. Every time he came to my flat, he would go into the bathroom to shoot up, sometimes alone, sometimes with other individuals he had brought with him who were just looking for a fix as well. With a sad heart, I told Cliffy that he could no longer come around and get off in my bathroom.

It was no surprise that he overdosed and died. It reminded me of a story he'd told me. Cliffy stated that while in the brig, he was observed by this guard, a southerner armed with a .45 pistol. He'd hold the pistol just so, polishing it or keeping it in his lap. He would begin to speak frightening things about "the Jews," as Cliffy was still Jewish at the time. I can only think that when this guard looked into Cliffy's eyes, he saw enough to realize he meant it. Cliffy may not have been the hardest guy I've ever met, but he was definitely the most fearless.

When I was twenty-one years old and had only recently begun working as an actor, I was asked to do a reading with Elia Kazan, arguably the world's most successful director on theater and screen, for a new film he was casting. It was called America, America, and it would follow the trip of a young Greek man to the United States. They were looking for a young, somewhat unknown actor with ethnic features to portray the lead part. I figured I had a shot. I'm not sure if I would have excelled at it, but I felt like I had a good shot because I met the description.

But I was late, so I missed the audition. When I arrived, they had already left, and the situation was finished. They got someone else. My first thought at that moment was not about me. Before I even went to the audition, I thought about how I would aid my mother. I would lift her out of poverty and despair, giving her everything she had always desired and needed. Not because it would imply I was successful. Not because she could have done more with the money. Because she would have attended it. It would have piqued her natural curiosity because she was intelligent. It would have given her a jumpstart. I believe she would have survived.

Outside the cab, I noticed their apartment lights were on. It was a little bigger than the former place. I walked up the stairs and through the door to find my grandma and grandfather, their eyes wet with sorrow. My mother was gone. You see, it was too late. I was too late. She had died, like Tennessee Williams, by choking on her own medications and regurgitating them, as so many others had. Many people wish to leave this world for a better one, and she was in a position where she might escape by using narcotics. Some believed she had committed suicide, something she had attempted nearly fifteen years before. But she didn't leave a note this time. She was just gone. That's why I've always left a question mark next to her death. When drugs are involved, people frequently die even if they had no intention of killing themselves. I'm not sure she did. To honor my mother's memory, I'd like to offer her the benefit of the doubt, and dignity.

When I was twenty-one years old and had only recently begun working as an actor, I was asked to do a reading with Elia Kazan, arguably the world's most successful director on theater and screen, for a new film he was casting. It was called America, America, and it would follow the trip of a young Greek man to the United States. They were looking for a young, somewhat unknown actor with ethnic features to portray the lead part. I figured I had a shot. I'm not sure if I would have excelled at it, but I felt like I had a good shot because I met the description.

But I was late, so I missed the audition. When I arrived, they had already left, and the situation was finished. They got someone else. My first thought at that moment was not about me. Before I even went to the audition, I thought about how I would aid my mother. I would lift her out of poverty and despair, giving her everything she had always desired and needed. Not because it would imply I was successful. Not because she could have done more with the money. Because she would have attended it. It would have piqued her natural curiosity because she was intelligent. It would have given her a jumpstart. I believe she would have survived.

Many people wish to leave this world for a better one. She was in a position where she might escape by using narcotics. Some believed she had committed suicide, something she had attempted nearly fifteen years before. But she didn't leave a note this time. She was just gone. That's why I've always left a question mark next to her death. When drugs are involved, people frequently die even if they had no intention of killing themselves. I'm not sure she did. To honor my mother's memory, I'd like to offer her the benefit of the doubt, and dignity. The next morning, I'll never forget seeing my grandfather sitting in a folding chair in the middle of the room, with nothing around him, stooped over with his head in his hands, almost between his legs. He just continued beating his foot against the floor. I'd never seen him like that. I had never seen my granddad that emotional before. He did not speak, but I understood what he was saying. No. This was the incorrect thing to do. She was too young. She could have gotten help. What a waste.

I worked as an usher at the Rivoli Theatre in Times Square. Others of the other guys who worked there were on the run, and others had families to maintain, so ushering was one of three jobs they were doing to feed their wives and children. Then I'd look at what I was holding and realize they'd given me a used match from a matchbook. I had to laugh.

At another job, I delivered Show Business newspapers to newsstands on Seventh Avenue. It was published once a week, and people in the industry would buy and read it to learn about which plays were being produced and where they could audition. This was invaluable information. I earned twelve dollars for one day of labor, which was a large sum to me. When I was paid, I'd go to the pub and spend my singles budget. I liked to roll my dollar notes into a large ball and peel them off one by one, like a big shot, before snapping them down on the counter like I had more where that came from. When you're down and out, you try to sleep until 4:00 p.m. to avoid hunger. If I could gather up $1.19 and spend it on a steak and a baked potato at Tad's Steaks, it would be like having Thanksgiving dinner.

I had a small red wagon that I used to transport the newspapers from Thirty-Fourth Street to Fifty-Seventh Street. In the rear of the wagon, I kept a bottle of Chianti wine. When it was pouring rain, they'd give me a head-to-toe poncho that didn't do anything for me, but it did protect the newspapers I was carrying.

With Charlie and Chekhov, I believe drinking saved my life. I was able to self-medicate. It helped me get through my agony and kept me away from Bellevue's outpatient clinic. I'd drink at night and then take drugs the next day to calm down. I was always trying to be quiet since my mind was racing, and alcohol had a relaxing effect. If I took cocaine, I would probably float, so I drank to relieve the agony and emptiness and diminish my energy. All I know is it worked for me. I had a detachment with Charlie, but I couldn't explain why. I'm not sure what I did or didn't do. It wasn't because we had argued. I believe Charlie recognized my potential, but he had his own life to cope with. He was in his mid-thirties, had a wife and a child, and was looking for something different. I was this child in my early twenties, sensitive and underdeveloped. I was almost hopeless. Perhaps I called him too frequently, or I was overly reliant on him. Perhaps he assumed that after losing my mother, I needed something different. But my degree of sophistication didn't match his. I was behind, and he was ahead.

I was feeling adrift and alone in the Village, consumed by my sentiments about my mother and a general malaise. Everything about my existence was fading. I got on a pay phone at a pub and called my grandfather in the Bronx to tell him what I was going through, and then I started crying. I had relocated out of the Bronx by then and found a low-rent rooming house in Chelsea for $8 per week. Another time, I called my grandfather after he had helped me find a job in construction. I had been up all night the night before I was meant to start, and I called him at 7 a.m. But I continued to do these other menial jobs. That was all I could accomplish. I lacked education and had no drive to obtain more. I was only interested in one thing. I thought I was an artist.

My grandfather died that same year, as is common when a parent loses a kid. My mother was his first kid, and they had a wonderful relationship; he loved her, and she loved her father—it was clear. I was still delivering Show Business newspapers at the time, and I passed out on the route. It must have been due to a lack of nourishment and the trauma of losing my grandfather.

He was a warm man with a sweetheart, despite coming from a harsh background. When his family relocated to East Harlem, where many Sicilians had settled, they lived amid criminals who had not yet become household names but were still renowned at the time. That world was available to my grandfather, but despite his poverty, he chose not to pursue it. As he once told me, he never had the heart to enter that underworld.

Chapter 3: A Tiger and an Indian

Herbert Berghof was slow to rage, and he was furious with me. All it took was watching me act. At HB Studio, it was customary for all acting schools to convene in a seminar room on occasion, with each teacher selecting one or two of their pupils to play a scene in front of Berghof. Being chosen was a source of pride, and the level of work was generally quite impressive.

Charlie had chosen me and a classmate to perform a brief scene from a teleplay called Crime in the Streets, about a gang of street youngsters. I'd worked on the scenario before in other acting workshops and with Charlie, so I felt comfortable with it. I wore a white tank top that I believed fit the character, and I gave the moment the intensity it needed. As an actor, your performance is always an expression of how you feel about things. Not only what's on the page, but how you're feeling right now—your difficulties, as we might call them today. And you don't always know how you feel until you're in the moment and say the lines. However, whatever you do is a representation of yourself. I was merely performing a scene that I felt expressed something about me, embodying a type of person I previously knew and a milieu in which I spent time.

I couldn't figure out what I did to make Berghof so emotional. He was a well-known actor and theatrical director who had directed the first Broadway production of Waiting for Godot, so his judgment was valued. Perhaps he immediately disliked me or my type. I appeared to have come in off the street. I have faced this type of bias in my life. The uncommon intensity of his answer lingered with me for decades. When I was in my seventies and Charlie was seriously ill with multiple sclerosis, I would go to his hospital in Santa Monica and sit by his bedside to chat to him. One day, I brought up what had transpired in the classroom all those years ago.

It was the early 1960s, and something was occurring in the acting world. I wondered if it was unfamiliar to someone like Herbert Berghof. Perhaps he didn't like my choice of subject, didn't relate to it personally, or didn't like how it was presented. Not only was my scene unfamiliar to him, but so were the selections he had seen other students do that day. Perhaps it wasn't such a shock to him after all. Perhaps individuals like him had watched the train approaching in the distance for some time, and now it had arrived at his door. It could have felt like a new chapter was about to begin, and it wouldn't include him.

It had begun with Brando. He was the influencer. The force. The originator. His collaborations with Tennessee Williams and Elia Kazan resulted in something more visceral. It was threatening. Brando had formed a trinity of actors, alongside Montgomery Clift and James Dean. Clift possessed beauty, emotion, and vulnerability. Dean was like a sonnet, compact and efficient, capable of accomplishing so much with the smallest gesture or nuance. And, if Dean was a sonnet, Brando was an epic poem. He had the look. He possessed charisma. He had talent.

However, evolution has always made humans nervous. There was hostility toward Brando. They said he murmured. They believed his looks were too gentle and delicate. They claimed he likes to show his chest. If people criticized his approach, it was because they did not understand the technique that went into it. But he discovered whatever it was that allowed him to express himself and communicate it to audiences in such a way that they could identify with him. Brando paved the way for the world's Paul Newmans, Ben Gazzaras, Anthony Franciosas, and Peter Falks, and John Cassavetes, who was his own unique phenomenon. These were the idols of a generation before mine, actors who had already left the studios and been out in the world for a decade or more by the time I arrived. And Dustin Hoffman opened the door for the performers.

At the age of twenty-five, I became a building superintendent owing to my boyhood friend Bruce from the South Bronx, who got me a job in a building on Sixty-Eighth Street and Central Park West. He was leaving to marry, and he knew I could use the work and a place to live, so I now had a home in a fantastic neighborhood. I was making $14 per week and had my own, rent-free apartment in the building. The flat was a little room with only my bed; when you opened the door, all you saw was a kitchen and a bathroom that was exposed to everyone. My apartment's window had bars on it, as in a prison, so if there was a fire, you couldn't escape. I knew I was not qualified for the position. Outside my apartment door, it said Super, so I got an 8 x 10 glossy photo of me and used Band-Aids to hang it above the sign. I got that image from Michael Avedon, a relative of photographer Richard Avedon, after he saw me in Creditors. He wanted to snap images of me so I could email them to agents and casting directors. It was a good shot of myself, so I put it up there not for anyone in the business to see, but for anyone who came to visit me to have a good laugh.

Penny Allen, Charlie's wife, would stop by the building and assist me by scrubbing the hallway floors on her hands and knees, knowing how desperately I needed a place of my own. I was going from one location to another, frequently landing on a friend's couch or floor. My super's apartment was just big enough to be alone with your thoughts. One Sunday at seven a.m., I heard a knock on the door. A nice elderly woman in her Sunday hat, probably on her way to the Christian Science church up the street, stood there looking at me. So I let her use my bathroom, which was in the kitchen and took up the other half of the apartment. After she concluded her thing, she said goodbye, no thank you, and no tip, and then she left me alone with a smell I had never felt before. I'm telling you, I've never smelled anything like it at a zoo. I needed to get out. The space was too small to accommodate it. I sat on a seat in Central Park West, looking melancholy and trying to get over this trauma.

Most of the time, I sat in that flat and played Mozart on an ancient phonograph. Charlie and Penny were on the outs for a while, so he'd stop by with their gorgeous daughter, Deirdre, and she'd bounce about on the bed while Charlie and I worked on beer bottles. Then, about two p.m., we'd all walk to the bar around the corner on Sixty-Ninth Street and get tiny Deirdre at Shirley Temple to drink while we continued to drink, quoting Chekhov, Dylan Thomas, and Eugene O'Neill. We couldn't remain very long because we couldn't afford it. Whatever task Charlie came to my house to accomplish, he never finished.

Sometimes the young women who resided in the building noticed my photograph on the door of my super's apartment. They would notice I was an actress and become interested in me. I was a young man who was not in a relationship at the time, and I would have brief affairs with them. One of the women I went out with was from the Midwest, a country gal. I'm not sure what brought her to New York, but she was quite lovely. After one of our flings, we cuddled together in my bed. The area was so little that I could stretch my arms out from the bed and almost touch both walls. You had to crawl in from the foot of the bed because there was no room on either side. We were just reclining there contentedly, looking up at the cracked and collapsing ceiling. The room was peaceful and quiet.

One day, I was at home in my superintendent's apartment, perhaps listening to Stravinsky with a Ballantine Ale in one hand and a languid cigarette in the other, when a man came over and handed me a script by Israel Horovitz. The Indian Wants the Bronx was a brief one-act play about an East Indian and two street toughs who meet on Upper Fifth Avenue. The Indian is seeking for his son, whose address and phone number he has on paper, but he's in the incorrect area of town and doesn't understand English. The street toughs have no interest in assisting the Indian; instead, they laugh and harass him. The play was unlike anything I'd read before. It felt mysterious and even dangerous—you could tell the Indian was out of his league, and something horrible was about to happen the moment he crossed paths with those two young lads. But at its core, it was a narrative about how people talk past each other and fail to connect. It was a wonderful and frequently humorous play.

Israel had heard of me through Tullio Garzone. Tullio was a friend of Penny Allen's, and he had previously directed my children's theater productions, such as The Adventures of High Jump. Penny recommended me for the first run of Israel's play, which he was now directing. Without Penny, there would be no Tullio. Without Tullio, there would be no The Indian Wants the Bronx for me, or any of the events that followed. But I didn't know any of that—all I knew was that Israel and Tullio wanted me to portray one of the toughs, a man dubbed Murph. He was a bit unusual, with an unpredictable personality. You saw him and thought, "He's capable of things we haven't seen before."

As an actor, I'd already portrayed a variety of unusual and exciting stage characters, including lowlifes, gamblers, artists, and warriors. In certain ways, your preparation for any portion remains consistent. You must organize yourself in such a way that you can bring yourself to the part. You must know someone else in yourself. And I suppose I have a lot of myself in me.

What actors call their instrument is their complete being, including their body and soul. It's what you play; it absorbs and releases things. And when I believe a position is appropriate, I don't have to do anything to produce a pleasing sound on my instrument. It will play, and the notes will simply appear. I'll also want to do it. I want to go there. I'd like to play my instrument because it'll just flow out. I saw it all in The Indian Wants the Bronx. It felt like something I'd actually experienced, and I could apply my entire life to it. I held the reins and could ride the horse. Murph was nearly a reincarnation of Cliffy and the rest of my team, and if I hadn't discovered acting, I might have ended up like him as well.

We staged readings of The Indian Wants the Bronx in Connecticut and then performed it in Provincetown at the Gifford House, which was so small that the audience had to walk through the stage to exit. They also did, sometimes right in the middle of the act. They walked so near to me that I could stick my leg out and trip them, but I never did. I stayed in character. The performance was just about an hour long and there was no intermission, so I'm not sure why they left, other than they didn't enjoy it.

When I was a messenger for Standard Oil in Rockefeller Center, I worked with a guy named John Cazale. He was a few years older than me, thin, and had a low-key demeanor. He was modest, but he also had a sense of reality and a solid understanding of how the world operated. He seems to know everything. My understanding of global politics was that Hitler was gone, which was positive. Aside from that, I had no idea what was happening. Johnny would read The New York Times, comprehend every topic, and explain it to me. He at least tried.

I'd been performing The Indian Wants the Bronx on and off for almost a year when they decided to move it from Broadway to the Astor Place Theatre. I was no longer doing the superintendent's job. I don't think I got fired—I just left and I don't know why. I had far too many strange experiences and escapades in that flat to recount. It was an era of awakening for me, and I remember it fondly. When I resigned that job, I left everything behind—all I had was a boiler permit and my first and only degree. I traveled into the provinces, this time to Boston, to join the circus of acting troupes and begin a career in repertory theater.

So, when I arrived in New York to interview Ruth Newton, I dressed like the character I was portraying in Boston: a three-piece blue suit, a shirt, and a tie. I assumed that was how you conducted things because I didn't know better. I drank a beer and headed to the theater for my audition. I sat in a basement chamber beneath the stage, where all of the other performers were waiting, including guys I knew from the performers Studio. As their names were called out one by one, they would come forward to read with a stage manager. My character looks up at a skyscraper across the street. It's the residence of his social worker, whom he's required to visit.

The first New York Times critic to write on The Indian Wants the Bronx didn't particularly appreciate it, and he didn't even mention the play's cast, all of whom he was unfamiliar with. But then came Clive Barnes, the Times' lead theater critic, who was British and noted for his taste and refinement. He gave me and the show such a positive evaluation that they began repeating it in commercials. As more people came to see it, news spread. Since Julian Beck and Judith Malina launched the Living Theatre, off Broadway has become much more fashionable and even profitable. It was never going to compete with Broadway, but you could make a decent living. Off Broadway was transitioning from its beatnik, bohemian vibe in the late 1950s and early 1960s to a more formalized style. John Cazale and I both won Obie Awards for the play, which are akin to Tony Awards for off-Broadway productions. That summer, we spent two weeks in Italy at the Spoleto Festival with The Indian Wants the Bronx. I would still be playing if I hadn't quit. For years afterward, I would have recurring dreams about performing or putting on The Indian Wants the Bronx. It had that much of an impression on me. It was my introduction to the world. Before that, I always felt as if I was on the outside looking in. The Indian Wants the Bronx was the climax of a life that began with my mother taking me to the movies as a child, since everything changed after that play.

Bregman's office glowed with prosperity. He sat behind a well-polished wooden desk, with the windows providing a panoramic view of Manhattan. He had a roster of celebrity clients that was quite intimidating. I was unsure where I fit in. He rose up to shake my hand, and I thought I noticed something: the glitter of a pearl handle on the side of his jacket. I noticed he had a gun. He had a license and retained it for his own safety because he walked with a severe limp. He suffered polio as a child, yet he never let it affect his life. I later learned he was involved in bootlegging as a young man. That was the word, anyway. I never asked.

Bregman possessed some of Gatsby's characteristics. He was a handsome man in his early forties with a very refined voice, but he spoke to me in a way that made me feel at ease. I would never borrow money from him—especially since he carries a gun. I didn't want that kind of duty. But when he stated that, I knew he was serious and would put his money where his mouth was. This was someone who had power and was willing to use it on my behalf. He would genuinely go the distance to support me.

When I moved to Boston to perform repertory theater, it was a new world for me. I began to broaden my perspective beyond New York and the small circle of off-off-Broadway influences that constituted my idea of theatre at the time. I had roles to play. I got paid and could eat. And I was out there with other repertory actors my age— about twenty-five or twenty-six—who seemed to know things I didn't. I had my dog-eared Chekhov books and classical recordings, but when they exposed me to the music of the Mamas and Papas, it felt like they were revealing a big cosmic secret.

Like Oedipus, I needed to know. I opened the paper and found a review of our show. And it virtually glowed off the paper. The lead actors were repeatedly complimented for their performances. There are also supporting actors. As I was reading this, I received my cue from the overhead speaker on the ceiling. That meant I had to go on stage. So I walked out in front of the audience, having read the worst criticism of my early career, and made my entrance laughing. A nice chuckle can help at times. I stopped reading reviews after that, but it

41

stayed with me. I still remember how it hurt. Another impression I had was fairly simple: This person must dislike me. That happens, and it is in the essence of the beast.

I performed better that season in America Hurrah at the same venue. Jean-Claude van Itallie wrote these three short plays, and I appeared in two of them. In one scene, I played an effeminate gym instructor who was quite pretentious and full of himself. It was a pretty humorous role. In the other segment, I played a nerdy TV ratings guy, alongside John Seitz and a young actress named Jill Clayburgh. It was a crazy comic piece, and I was enjoying my role, so I simply went with it. Around 1:00 or 2:00 a.m. one night, after the pubs had closed, we ventured out to Gloucester, drunker than skunks, thanks to the kindness of someone sober enough to take us there. There was a rock formation that overlooked the ocean, and at some predawn hour, I found myself drunkenly scrambling my way up these rocks, risking my life since I knew Jill and her friend Jennifer Salt would be there after me doing whatever I did. The crevasses had begun to twist and turn, so I waited on a peak overlooking the ocean, wondering who would appear next.

I'd been in relationships with women before, but none compared to my romance with Jill, which was our version of what we believed a romance looked like at the time. She was four years younger than me, but we were both in our twenties, just starting in the world of professional acting. In other respects, we couldn't have been more dissimilar—two inhabitants of the same city who had experienced it in very different ways. She was an Upper East Sider through and through, having attended a private secondary school and Sarah Lawrence College. Many things were about to happen to me, and she had a significant impact on my happiness during them. I'm not sure I was good for her, but she was surely good for me. People, like everything else, become more valuable as you grow further away from them. And with her, all I saw was her worth. She made me joyful. And we knew we cared for one another.

I was once invited to Los Angeles to meet with Franco Zeffirelli, the legendary director of Romeo and Juliet, who was casting for a new picture. He was looking for young men, but I was twenty-seven and surrounded by kids auditioning for the same role as me. I may have appeared young, but when compared to a seventeen-year-old, the situation changes dramatically. Zeffirelli had no idea who I was, and he spent the entire session lecturing to me about Method acting in a way that gave me the sense he didn't care about it or me—all while filming me.

I've always been asked what Method acting was and what the Actors Studio does, and I've never been able to answer right. I can explain what the Actors Studio is. It is not a school; rather, it is a venue where professional actors can come to hone their craft without paying a fee. To speak in front of a moderator—who may be anyone from Lee Strasberg to Paul Newman to Ellen Burstyn—and an audience of your peers and receive criticism without being criticized or becoming rude. A forum for actors, directors, and writers to interact with other artists. No one expects anything from you but to find. You could create a scenario from a play or a movie that no one else would allow you to do on stage, and then move it from the Studio to the real world. Or you could sit there for years without performing, just attending. Imagine you're out of job, pounding the pavement, or alone in your room, and you come upon something like this. The place itself keeps the spirit of what you're doing alive.

I spent a few more days in LA, where I knew no one. I wandered around and ended up in a hotel room with half a pint of something, staring at the Hollywood sign, which began to conjure up images of Cary Grant dancing with Gina Lollobrigida, Boris Karloff eating a pumpkin, and Bette Davis and Greta Garbo singing a duet of "Hooray for Hollywood."

In this profession, you go up, down, and back up again. I went to work for Joe Papp on a play called Hui Hui. Joe Papp was one of my heroes. He made significant contributions to Shakespeare in New York with his Shakespeare in the Park summer program. He was a rare theatrical dynamo, and his death left a hole that has yet to be filled. I felt it was terrific to be working with Joe, whom I loved, and the play was rather good. However, he believed I was taking too long to respond. Papp did not have the patience. Charlie Durning, the famous actor who was in the play with me, begged Joe to let me continue in it with him, but to no avail. So here I was, after my great success in Indian, getting fired for the next thing I accomplished. Talk about sobering up. In a way, it was a break. I was used to the highs and lows of showbiz. It is an experience shared by all actors.

My next project came about when actor William Devane left his position in Don Petersen's play Does a Tiger Wear a Necktie?. He departed to do another program, and I was offered the role. Tiger was, in some ways, unremarkable. I had sort of been there, done that. The drama was inspired by social themes, particularly prevalent concerns about drugs at the time. It depicted the story of a group of adolescents who were recovering and relapsing addicts at a city rehab center. I portrayed another tough character, Bickham, a wild-eyed addict with a hair trigger. Unlike Murph, he was a complete loner who was determined to remain that way.

When I read for the director, Michael Schultz, and reached that line, I burst into tears. I fell apart when I had to pronounce those words. It was quite difficult for me to express. Everyone was quiet. They recruited me for it. I never had a breakdown after that. No matter how many times I played that scene in the play, I never sobbed again. It never got as far as it did the first time I read it. I was playing the character, but I rejected it since I hadn't prepared well. I did not want to go there every night. I was able to do it without feeling it; I had devised a strategy to make it appear like I did. Something happens throughout the repetition of performance that eventually starts to work for you rather than against you. But I wasn't paying attention to the repetitions because we didn't know how long the play would go, and it didn't—it ended after about a month. During that period, the great Sidney Poitier came to see me in the play. Poitier was on top of the world, and when he came into my dressing room, he was literally beaming. He was quite kind, but I could see he wanted to say something to me. He could see I needed to chat to someone about my future and what it could be like. He wasn't critical; he was really encouraging, and he told me about it in a very delicate way. It was all subtext, but it was also quite nice and generous.

Tiger marked my Broadway debut, and it ran in the Belasco Theater, which seemed like a dream come true. A few blocks away, in one direction, stood the ancient Rivoli Theatre, where I had worked as an usher. In another way was the High School of Performing Arts, from which I had not yet graduated. Buildings and offices surrounded me, where I had previously worked as a messenger and other low-level positions. I was back on my native turf. When Tiger received a Tony Award nomination, I invited Marty Bregman to attend the ceremony. I was up against some really strong competition. I thought my chances of winning were nil to none, and I hadn't written a speech.

I didn't consider myself very successful, but I suppose I was beginning to make a reputation for myself in the show world. I was messing about on a leased piano, attempting to compose my own music, something I thought I had a talent for at the time. For a while, I believed I was the reincarnation of Beethoven or Satie, whom I adore. I wanted to be Beethoven, but everything that came out sounded like Satie to my obtuse musical ear. In the midst of my artistic endeavor, I was stopped by a call from that actor from The Wicked Cooks, the guy with the lisp, whom I had attempted to understudy with Martin Sheen. I wasn't sure how he acquired my phone number. It had been a few years after my little appearance in that play, and he always treated me as if I were well below earth. He began to make small talk, but it felt strange. I wondered what this guy was calling. Oh. I see. This guy wants something from me. He believes I'll get him a job now that I'm nearing celebrity status. He believes I'm becoming a big shot.

Chapter 4: The New World

My association with the filmmaker who would change my life began unexpectedly. Francis Ford Coppola had seen me on Broadway when I performed Does a Tiger Wear a Necktie?, but we had not met at the time. He was a young director with a few films under his belt. He unexpectedly sent me an original script he had written, a great love story about a young college professor with a wife and children who falls in love with one of his pupils. It was mystical and bizarre, but well written. Francis wanted to speak with me about portraying the professor. That required me to board an aircraft and travel to San Francisco, which I would find challenging. I didn't like flying. I wondered, is there another way to get there? I can't ask him to come all the way to New York, can I? I bit the bullet and went.

It was my first time in San Francisco, and I was simply grateful to be there at the invitation of someone as great as Francis. He was like a college professor, an intellectual with a bushy beard, a toothy smile, and a scarf wrapped around his neck in Fellini style. For the next five days and nights, he took me to dinner and we discussed his film project over bottles of wine. I believed Francis had been touched by genius. He was excited. He was a leader, a doer, and a risk taker.

He took me to his company, American Zoetrope, which was located in a large building—basically an above-ground bunker where he worked among a diverse group of people. If I remember well, I believe I saw George Lucas and Steven Spielberg there. Martin Scorsese and Brian De Palma were also in the cast. I wasn't sure who they were at the time, but I knew they weren't actors. They were a group of young revolutionaries from the 1960s who were set to take filmmaking into the 1970s. They were aware of larger developments in the film culture.

But I was an unknown, and the film Francis wanted to make with me was rejected everywhere, never to be produced. And I went home, thinking I'd never hear from him again. Months passed, and one day in the middle of the day, I received a phone call. On the other end of the line, I recognized a name and voice from the past: Francis Coppola.

When I think about it, I had no interest in show business, and I have no idea why. I knew acting would be my career, but the entire industry eluded me and my lifestyle. I did not live in Los Angeles, where it was concentrated. I was in New York, and things were going my way on the island of Manhattan. I was a theatrical enthusiast. I had my Tony and Obie Awards, the performers Studio, and a group of fellow performers. Hollywood was a faraway location, and film was a different universe than theater. And you do it while covered in cables and facing a camera, with a crowd of people breathing and coming into your field of vision. Oh, and I forgot about the smoke—they smoke up the room, which I assume is for the camera. The difference between film and stage acting was like being on a high wire. In film acting, the wire is on the floor; you can always return and try something else. Acting on stage takes place thirty feet above ground level. If you don't make it, you'll fall. This is the difference in the amount of adrenaline required to be a theater actor.

My first film part came not from Marty Bregman, but from a fantastic casting director named Marion Dougherty, who had previously worked on Midnight Cowboy and had seen me in The Indian Wants the Bronx. She offered me a one-day role in Patty Duke's coming-of-age comedy, Me, Natalie, in which I would portray a guy she meets at a dance party. Patty was the loveliest person I knew. However, the entire situation was catastrophic and depressing for me. I arrived early since I had been told to do so, before everyone else did. I had no one to talk to, so I sat and waited. And waited.

I did not make another film for nearly two years. Marty Bregman had worked to build the panic in Needle Park, which I witnessed. The screenplay, written by John Gregory Dunne and Joan Didion, was based on a true story of two adolescent heroin users, one male and one female, who fall in and out of love amid drug scarcity. Marty also represented its director, Jerry Schatzberg, who was better known as a photographer and hadn't done much in cinema before, and they both preferred me for the role of the character named Bobby. I figured I could play it. A couple people could have done it, but it was a role that I could easily cast. I'd made my theatrical bones portraying these types of street characters, so I was grateful to have that option for my first film. The college professor position that Francis offered me was certainly a bit of a stretch, but I like the role. I believe that's what it boils down to.

If I have a sense about a part, it is worthwhile for me to try. When I had my final audition to join the Actors Studio, I was delighted for the opportunity to play two different characters that night. One was taken from Elmer Rice's Counsellor at Law, and the other from Hugh Wheeler's Look, We've Come Through. In the first, I portrayed an angry communist zealot, a revolutionary, in a scene with Owen Hollander as an attorney. In the other, I portrayed a gay streetwalker in a sequence alongside Nathan Joseph. I auditioned with two guys who were pals back then. The personas I played in those two moments were very distinct, and I believe this helped the judges, who included Elia Kazan, Harold Clurman, and Lee Strasberg. Seeing the diversity of the personalities, who couldn't have been more different, may have given them cause to take a chance on me.

When you're a young actor with absolutely no film experience and are offered a main role in The Panic in Needle Park, you reply, "Okay, I'll jump through that hoop." However, there were some obstacles I couldn't overcome. I believed I had the role, but as they say, the papers hadn't been signed, so the part wasn't mine just yet. Meanwhile, someone asked me to do a play reading since another actor was absent and they wanted someone to fill in for one of the leads. It was a character I was unfamiliar with, therefore I would be doing a cold reading with no preparation before reading it to an audience.

We were up on stage. The players were receiving their scripts, and I was gazing down at the pages, hoping to see the name of the character I was supposed to play. The crowd was nearly full, but I noticed a few folks who did not appear to belong there. To my amazement, one of them was Nick Dunne, Panic's producer, together with his brother John Gregory Dunne and Joan Didion, who co-wrote the script. They entered with a few more folks I didn't recognize. I was shocked. You have to understand that I was never asked to audition for Panic; I was offered the role. Now, if they suddenly expected me to audition for it, I wouldn't want them to give me a final pass at a cold reading of a play I had never seen before.

The Panic in Needle Park was my showcase. It is still acclaimed today, and Jerry Schatzberg performed an outstanding job. I truly enjoyed working with Kitty Winn, who played my lover and co-addict. We didn't understand each other, yet we got along. Sometimes she'd give me a puzzled expression when I said something. I would say anything, and I had no idea what she was thinking. I had no idea who she was. And that was fine. She received Best Actress at the Cannes Film Festival for The Panic in Needle Park. She went on to star in The Exorcist and a few other films before retiring from acting. She was a very engaging and nice person to be around, pleasant without being overpowering. But she didn't enjoy the company and couldn't handle some of what was going on. Everybody has a dark secret.

Paramount had previously rejected Francis' whole cast. They turned down Jimmy Caan and Bob Duvall, two well-established performers who were on their way to becoming stars. They renounced Brando for Christ's sake. When I walked into the studio, it was obvious they did not want me either. And I knew I wasn't the only one under consideration. Many of the young actors of the day were auditioning for Michael. That was an awful sensation. But The Panic at Needle Park was what pushed me over the brink. Panic had not yet been released, but Jerry Schatzberg provided Paramount with eight minutes of film from my performance, which helped convince the studio to take a bet on me.

The Godfather book was a big success, so everyone was talking about it and enthusiastic about the upcoming picture. Francis drove me to a barbershop in San Francisco before my screen test, because he wanted Michael to have an authentic 1940s haircut. When the barber heard we were filming, he took a step back, took it all in, and began shivering. We later discovered he had a heart attack. Behind the scenes, word spread that there was a lot at stake for this project. Paramount execs were upset with one another and engaged in yelling confrontations. You could feel the stress everywhere. So I performed my Zen "this too shall pass" thing. I told myself, "Go to the character."

I sat through a few days of screen testing in an early version of Michael's army outfit, with a hangdog expression on my face. I've always had that appearance. I believe it was a facade I kept up because it got me through everything. But I must confess that the scene I was requested to perform was not the best one they could have chosen. In the opening wedding scene, Michael explained to his girlfriend, Kay, what his family actually did and who all the players were in his father's operation. It was a banal scene of exposition, simply myself and Diane Keaton sitting at a drab little table, drinking glasses of water that we thought were wine while I lectured about Sicilian wedding traditions. The role's influence could not be fully realized. My understanding of Michael was similar to planting a garden; it would take some time in the story for the flowers to bloom.

But here's a secret: Francis wanted me. He wanted me, and I knew it.

There's nothing like being wanted by a filmmaker. It's the best thing an actor could ever have. He also handed me a gift: Diane Keaton. He had a few girls auditioning for the role of Kay, but the fact that he chose to pair me with Diane indicated she had an advantage in the process. I knew she was successful in her career, having appeared on Broadway in productions such as Hair and Play It Again, Sam with Woody Allen. I met Diane at a pub in Lincoln Center a few days before the screen test, and we hit it off immediately. She was easy to chat to and funny, and she felt I was also hilarious. I immediately felt like I had a buddy and an ally.

I still needed to figure out who Michael was to me. Before production began, I would take lengthy walks up and down Manhattan, from Ninety-First Street to the Village and back, simply thinking about how I was going to portray him. I usually went alone, but occasionally I'd meet Charlie downtown and we'd stroll back uptown together. Michael begins as a familiar young man, getting by, a touch loopy and lumpy. He is simultaneously present and absent. It's all leading up to the moment when he offers to take out Sollozzo and McCluskey, the drug dealer and corrupt cop who colluded to murder Michael's father. He suddenly experiences a large explosion.

Before we began filming The Godfather, I met with little Al Lettieri, a superb actor who would portray Sollozzo. I understood what he meant, so I agreed with him. One day, we drove to a suburb just outside the city. Little Al led me to a traditional, attractive, and well-maintained home. You pass these kinds of homes all the time on your way from where you are to where you need to go, and you never think about who lives there. He led me inside and introduced me to the house leader, who appeared to be a typical businessman. I could have assumed he was a Wall Street executive, an investment banker, or a hedge fund manager. I shook his hand and said hello, and he was quite welcoming. He had a wonderful family. His wife offered us beverages and light appetizers on excellent porcelain. He had two small sons my age. I was just a mad actress who had come into his house to absorb as much as possible. Our chat remained courteous and surface-level. I never questioned Little Al why he had brought me here, but I considered what he had said before we arrived, and how this visit would help with what I was working on. Little Al knew a few males. Some actual men. And now he is presenting me to one of them.

I was a South Bronx kid. I am Italian. I am also a Sicilian. I knew what it was like to be assumed to have some sort of involvement with organized crime. Any name that concluded with a vowel was investigated for potential links to that world. Instead of being likened to Joe DiMaggio, you were linked with Al Capone. Most of us will never be victims or perpetrators. Nonetheless, we are captivated by these folks who are determined not to follow societal norms and are forging their own path. The outlaw is a distinctively American type of character. We grew up pretending to be Jesse James or Billy the Kid. They were folk heroes. They become part of our folklore. The Mafia's past is also part of that lore. Diane and I spent those initial days laughing with each other, having to recreate that opening wedding exposition scenario from the screen test that we despised so much. We were convinced we were in the worst film ever made based just on that one scene. Once we finished shooting for the day, we would return to Manhattan and get drunk. We felt our careers were over.

Back in Hollywood, Paramount began to look at the picture that Francis had filmed, and they once again questioned if I was the ideal actor for the role. Word had spread around the set that I was going to be let go from the picture. You could sense the loss of momentum as we shot. People were uncomfortable, including the crew, while I was working. I was very aware of it. The rumor was that I would be fired, as was the director. Not that Francis wasn't cutting it; I wasn't. But he was the one who made sure I was in the film.

I felt out of place in this role, but I also felt like I belonged there—a bizarre combination of emotions. Nobody wants to be somewhere they aren't wanted. Perhaps it would have been easier for me to leave and avoid the discomfort. What if they fired me? Would I have felt like I had missed out on something? Probably, but I've lost out on stuff before and recovered. I did not think it was important to have a career. I never thought about a career.

Finally, Francis decided something had to be done. One night, he invited me to meet him at the Ginger Man, a restaurant and watering hole for thirsty Lincoln Center types, where actors, dancers, maestros, and stagehands congregated at the bar. I went to a screening room the next day. I'd already been advised that I might be leaving the film. And as I looked at the video, which was all from early in the film, I said, "I don't think there's anything spectacular here." I wasn't sure what to do. However, the impact was just what I was looking for. I did not want to be noticed.

My entire objective for Michael was to demonstrate that he was oblivious of the situation and lacked a charismatic personality. My assumption was that this guy appeared out of nowhere. That was the strength of the characterisation. That was the only way this could work: the emergence of this individual, the finding of his abilities and potential. And, as you'll note, he's still not quite Michael when he enters the hospital to save his father. Even then, he only becomes Michael when he notices that Enzo the baker, whom he has been assigned to stand with outside the hospital and pretend to have a pistol, is shaking while he is not. By the end of the film, I hoped to have produced an enigma. I believe Francis was also hoping for this. However, neither of us understood how to communicate it to each other.

It was always assumed that Francis restructured the filming schedule to give the doubters in Hollywood a reason to believe in me and keep me in the film. The judgment is still out on whether he did it on purpose, and Francis has denied that he arranged it for my benefit, but he did speed up the filming of the Italian restaurant scene, in which the untested Michael arrives to exact retribution on Sollozzo and McCluskey. That scene wasn't supposed to be filmed until a few days later, but if something hadn't happened to allow me to demonstrate my abilities, there might not have been a later for me.

Sterling and Al Lettieri kept my spirits up. They set the tone and served as my role models. I looked to them as people who knew what to do and how to conduct themselves, and they welcomed me as a fellow actor. But finally, the script required me to excuse myself to use the restroom, locate a hidden gun, and blow their brains out. Then I had to rush out of the restaurant and escape by getting onto a moving automobile. There was no stand-in. I didn't have a stuntman. I had to do it myself. I jumped, but missed the car. Now I was laying in a gutter on White Plains Road in the Bronx, flat on my back and gazing up at the sky. My ankle had twisted so terribly that I couldn't move.

They recorded the rest of the car-jumping action with an unexpected stuntman, and they administered cortisone into my ankle until I was able to stand on my own two feet. Then Francis showed the restaurant scene to the studio, and they noticed something there. They retained me in the picture due to the scene I just performed. So I wasn't dismissed from The Godfather. I just kept doing what I was doing, thinking about during those lonely trips up and down the length of Manhattan. I did have a plan, a direction that I truly believed was the best way to proceed with this guy. And I was sure Francis felt the same way.

It took work to turn me into Michael Corleone. I needed to be presentable, which did not come easily to me. They pressured me to appear presentable. I'd come in every morning to play Michael, and

I'd show up with two or three different faces. One on each side of my head, with a third in the center. Some nights, I had very little or no sleep at all. Other times, I drank so much and consumed so much that my face became crooked. Dick Smith, the legendary makeup artist, had to put my face back together. And by the time I stepped out of his makeup chair, I had transformed into Michael.

My co-stars were very supportive. Almost nobody knew who I was. When no one is trying to impress you, you can see who people truly are. They could tell I was struggling and were extremely reassuring to me. Actors are sensitive people, therefore they will be more aware of how you feel. They have feelings. Your life is spent feeling everyone's emotions so you can play your character. The actors I've seen who are particularly talented have erect antennae. I felt it most strongly from John Cazale, whom I had a history with and considered a close friend, and Jimmy Caan. The script had assigned them the positions of my older brothers and counselors in the film, but they assumed those roles spontaneously via their interactions with me. They were intuitively protective and refused to let me fail. There were also Bob Duvall, Richard Castellano, Abe Vigoda, and everyone else who was completely supportive of me. I felt genuinely appreciated, which is beneficial in any situation.

Marlon was also generous to me, but I don't believe he kept everything for me because he shared it with the public. It's what made his performance memorable and endearing. We all fantasize about having someone like Don Vito to turn to. Many individuals get abused in this world, but if you have a Godfather, you can go to him and he would take care of it. That is why people react to him in the film. It was more than simply bluster and bravery; it was the humanity beneath it. That's why he had to play Vito larger-than-life, with his physical bulk, shoe polish in his hair, and cotton in his cheeks. His Godfather had to be an icon, and Brando created him as memorable as Citizen Kane, Superman, Julius Caesar, or George

Washington.

But Francis had a lot on his shoulders, as I found out while we were working on Vito's funeral sequence. We shot a massive sequence on Long Island that required a significant number of cast members and took a couple of days. The light was setting and I heard "Wrap! Wrap!" They told me I was finished for the day. So naturally, I'm pleased because I get to return home and have some fun, whatever that means. I was on my way to my trailer, thinking to myself, Well, I didn't fuck up too badly. I had no queues or obligations, which was fine.

You never know if a film will be fantastic. You know what? If it's a very fantastic script—and Mario and Francis wrote a really terrific script—there is a chance. An actor appears and plays his job, but the film is all about what occurs next, how an editor stitches it together, and how the director decides on the storyline. But there in that graveyard, I thought: If Francis is this passionate about it, then something is working. I knew I was in good hands.

Making the video took me to Sicily for the first time in my life. I wasn't prepared for it. It felt like a major hassle. And once I arrived, I was overcome by a sense of cosmic energy. Everything came flooding back to me, including things I'd never experienced. The paths that led to my being began here; everything I was or would become was in some way due to this location. It was eye-opening, consciousness-raising, and completely transformative. As an actor, you're constantly looking for identity and something to connect with. When I returned from the trip, I found myself urging everyone I knew that they should visit the places where their families came from and trace their ancestry back as far as they could. It's a means of checking in with reality, a reminder that you existed and will continue to exist.

I didn't know anyone in Sicily, and the locals didn't know me. They had no idea what part I played in The Godfather or that I was Sicilian. I was an unknown actor, and that was a pleasure. I never spoke with anyone. I didn't know what to talk about. But everywhere I went, the locals were fascinated and friendly to me. They didn't have much, but they were generous and gracious, and they'd ask a youngster from the film, or anyone else, to come in and eat with them in their small homes. I'd sit in solitude and consume the food they served.

When it came time to film the wedding scene, in which Michael marries Apollonia in a lovely ceremony, I stood there in my wool suit, next to Simonetta Stefanelli, who played my bride, and a large group of Italians who didn't know English. This didn't appear to be the most difficult sequence to film, but Francis had a bullhorn in his hand and was shouting commands to me. This scene brings back happy memories for me. He was a director working on a film, and I was an actor who couldn't do the majority of what he asked. But I danced my way through the ceremony, double-talked Italian to the folks there, and drove down the slope three or four feet. That's why we all enjoy movies. Anything's conceivable.

It got really hot in July. All of us wore wool. We were recording a sequence that required a large group of extras to form a line when a lunch break was called, and people began to disperse. I saw the invisible whip being cracked again, much like the director from The Wicked Cooks, and it bothered me. They had been standing in the heat since early morning. One of the men on the line raised his hand, shouted something in Italian, and pointed to his watch, which indicated that it was approximately two p.m. The extra was a short, slender man with gray hair and an attractive face. I believe he was in his seventies. He was modest. He simply shrugged his shoulders and went away. He left the picture, meaning he would not be compensated.

I loved him. I imagined what it was like to be him. What bravery.

These were poor folks who were paid a small amount to assist fill in the film's background. This guy doesn't have any money and is going away since he needs to go to lunch. He's going to get some cheese and a small piece of fruit. I previously had that freedom. But I did not want to switch places with the guy. I was simply reveling in the illusion that he had inspired. I saw him and thought, "That's something I agree on." In Spirit. For me, he was a hero.

When I completed making The Godfather, I was broke. I never had money, but suddenly I owed money. My manager and agents received compensation cuts, while I had to rely on Jill Clayburgh for help. Jill and I were home in our apartment one day when we heard a knock on the door. I opened it to discover a man handing me an envelope with a notice of service. And I wondered, What is this? While I was waiting to be hired for The Godfather, MGM cast me in another gangster film, a Mafia comedy called The Gang That Couldn't Shoot Straight, and now they were after me. It was like I was a player and the bookies were going to get me. I needed to engage lawyers to help me get out of that deal. I soon owed the lawyers $15,000 too.

I couldn't afford to continue the dispute with MGM, so I asked the head of their studio to meet me at the Pulitzer Fountain outside the Plaza Hotel on Fifty-Ninth Street and Fifth Avenue. It was a busy place, full of crazy and cool people on their lunch break, adult guys in hats and suits rushing to work, and mothers walking strollers. We sat on the brink of the fountain. I wasn't as strong as Vito or Michael Corleone, and their negotiating talents hadn't rubbed off on me. I begged him.

Before The Godfather's New York premiere, I had only seen it once, a few months ago, when Francis showed me an unfinished edit. At the end of the screening, I gave Francis feedback on my performance, and he looked at me with a look of disgust. Of course, when I look at an incomplete film, I can't help but see things I would do better. But you'd think I'd realize it wasn't my place to say this to the film's director, who had just spent the last year of his life dangling from the brink of a cliff by his fingernails to make it happen. I was insensitive: he had the elegance to show it to me, and I came in concerned about my performance rather than the excellent film he had created. As a young actor, you can be quite unconscious at times. You're preoccupied with other things, and your vain instincts and dumb ego render all types of elegance and decorum obsolete. I've seen it in others, I must admit. I hope I'm not still that way, but the verdict is out on that one.

I attended the premiere of The Godfather at the Loew's State Theatre in Times Square while wearing a bow tie the size of my head. I took Jill, my grandmother, my aunt, and my cousin Mark, who was basically my brother. It was like attending a ship's christening: stilted and strangely formal. All that was missing was someone smashing a bottle of champagne across the bow. I simply recall standing on a platform with my costars and being asked questions by the press that I couldn't answer. Then we took our seats, but I did not watch the movie. I did not want to see the end product. As soon as the lights went out, I left.

You know, I had a variety of feelings about myself in regard to movies. I couldn't watch myself on screen when others were watching me. It was weird and made me feel shy and humiliated. As a young performer, I suppose I needed but did not want attention. I understand it's a bit of a paradox, therefore I tried not to put myself in that scenario. Thankfully, I have changed. It's similar to how I overcame my fear of flying: I simply stopped caring.

I went virtually my whole life without watching The Godfather in its entirety. I'm not sure why. Perhaps I felt that because I was in it, I wouldn't be an appropriate audience. Of course, over the years, I'd see bits and pieces of it on TV, and once you're hooked, it's difficult to stop watching. But then I saw The Godfather at a showing commemorating its 50th anniversary at the Dolby Theatre in Hollywood, where a restored print was wonderfully projected with clear, excellent sound. The whole experience was quite encouraging. There isn't a single scene in the picture that doesn't have two or three things going on. There are no dull moments; it is continuously conveying a story. There was so much that I was struck. Take the scenario where Don Vito leaves the hospital after being shot. Marlon is on his bed, with the children's get-well cards all over him. And Robert Duvall, Jimmy Caan, and a few other males are gathered around the bed. They tell him Michael killed Sollozzo and had to flee to Sicily. The angle from which the scene is taken is fantastic. Brando's face is depressed as he turns his head and gestures his hand, indicating that he has heard enough. Dick Smith performed such an excellent job with Marlon's makeup that you can literally see marks on Brando's face; you can tell he's gone through a lot, and you can feel the monumental mountain that has been scaled. These things get under your skin because they were so well-planned and meticulously executed. They arranged that shot in such a way that it conveys all of the necessary information. That type of scene occurs frequently throughout the film.

However, when the film was released in 1972, I felt an immediate impact. It occurred at light speed. Everything changed. A few weeks after its release, I was strolling down the street when a middle-aged woman approached me and kissed my hand, calling me "Godfather." Because the film had only recently been released, I went about my usual routine as if nothing had changed. One day, I was standing at a curb waiting for the light to change, and this lovely redhead joined me. And I just went, "Whoa." Oh, my God. I'm not safe. Anonymity, sweet pea, the light of my existence, my survival tool—it's gone. You don't appreciate it until you've lost it.

Chapter 5: Grown-ups Don't Do Things Like This

Fame, as my buddy Heathcote Williams put it, is the perversion of the inherent human desire for affirmation and attention. It was transitory and odd. As an actor, I had been trying to shed light on the individuals I was observing and the roles I was portraying. Instead, it felt like all of the lights were glaring on me, and I couldn't see outside. I understand that we live in a different era, and that fame has a different connotation, but it impacted me hard a half-century ago. There are few things more dull than a famous person complaining about fame, so I won't dwell on it, even though I'm tempted.

I saw a picture of myself in the papers only once before doing The Godfather. It happened while I was in The Indian Wants the Bronx. I was in Montauk with Marty Bregman and a top New York elected politician. The next day, I'm reading The New York Times and came across a photo of the three of us—Marty Bregman, this white-haired guy from the government, and me. I was wearing a Russian hat and walked with a cane due to a knee injury. I was unable to gain perspective on what I was looking at. Nowadays, fame means something different. People desire it, and they go after it. They assume it's similar to winning the lotto. However, you pay for it in other ways. My reaction to its popularity was to remove myself from the film and the role I played in it. I inserted a wedge between it and me. I assured myself I had nothing to do with it. I knew there was a fantastic part for me, so I played it. But I had Coppola, and he is a miracle. He made that film.

I was wary of the media attention that comes with film roles. When I started repertory theater, I saw my future. These playwrights were prophets, and their plays had the potential to change my life. They improved my acting skills, provided me with an education, expanded my worldview, and made me happy. I'd end up marrying a seamstress and have ten children. It was a bizarre fantasy, but it gave me hope. I said as much in an interview with The New York Times before The Godfather elevated me to stardom. Years pass, and opinions shift, which is why having an opinion seems foolish. But the basic line is that I meant it then, and if given the opportunity, I would say it again. Perhaps eight kids instead of ten.

But I wouldn't end up living that life with Jill. She was a brilliant actress who was getting more work—we were frequently apart before The Godfather made me famous overnight. Our relationship did not terminate with frantic shouting and vehement disagreement. We liked each other and had been together about five years. She went on to make her own films, becoming well-known a few years later with An Unmarried Woman, which she directed for Paul Mazursky. She and I lived in the same neighborhood and frequently ran into one other, so we maintained a somewhat continuous contact. We remained friends, and our feelings were always present.

Meanwhile, The Godfather followed me wherever I went, overshadowing everything I did. I was shy about it, but the world wouldn't let me be. The uproar completely confused me. After The Godfather, they'd let me play anything. I was offered the Han Solo role in Star Wars. So, here I am, reading Star Wars. I gave it to Charlie. Get anyone but me. Sometimes I think, "At least look at the part." Maybe if I work on it, it will come together—you can get there. The whole objective of acting classes, the Actors Studio, and repertory theater was to choose roles that I didn't really feel qualified for. Sometimes my intellect requires expansion. Maybe I'll strike a connection in a role; I won't know unless I try. But there are instances when I simply say, "Wow, I really want to do that." Forget about "can" and "cannot"—that's different. Sometimes I get a part and have a feeling for it, and something goes boom-ba-boom inside and around me. I truly like that. I want to do it. But this happens as infrequently as I get a toothache.

I was offered the role of Billy the Kid in Sam Peckinpah's Pat Garrett and Billy the Kid. I adored Peckinpah. One of the best directors ever. Could you imagine acting in a movie alongside Bob Dylan? Who wouldn't want to play Billy the Kid? I assumed that was something I could do. Then I read the script and decided to perform some rewrites, fixing the script with Peckinpah, as I typically do with directors. I could almost picture it. I thought, "I'm not getting on any horses." They are overly huge. I'll be in Mexico with Peckinpah, and I'll most likely die from alcohol poisoning due to the amount of time I spend around it. And I passed on it. But I couldn't keep drinking and having fun forever. I wouldn't even call it enjoyable, simply being unconscious. At some point, I needed to do something different.

I stood in a field in Bakersfield, California. The temperature felt like 120 degrees to me. I'm seeing Gene Hackman descend down a sandy white hill the size of a mountain. It was a stunning photograph: a steel-gray sky overhead, untouched grasslands in front of him, and a single tree on the summit. Gene moved so slowly that the scene in front of me didn't seem to change. I could have been staring at a work of art. It took him a few minutes to descend this slope and slip through a chicken-wire fence that surrounded the field. Despite the heat, he's wearing three coats and other layers of clothing below since his persona is a vagrant who prefers to stay warm. while the audience sees this scene later, they won't realize how hot it was outside while we shot it. And once Gene finished this routine, he needed to record another take, so he'd turn around, go back up the hill, and walk back down.

I certainly did not want to play Scarecrow, my first cinematic part since The Godfather. I'd grown accustomed to New York and did not want to leave the city or my little group of pals. But Charlie read Garry Michael White's screenplay about a few drifters traveling across the country. It was a mix of Waiting for Godot and Of Mice and Men, and he thought it was a nice read. Jerry Schatzberg directed it, and I had previously worked with him on The Panic in Needle Park, which was excellent. And I would co-star with Gene Hackman, who had recently won an Oscar for The French Connection. I'm not sure if I purposefully chose something so different from The Godfather, something modest and small to get away from the glare of the spotlight. However, the character I was portraying, a fellow wanderer named Lion, was a touch eccentric and foolish. He was a poor boy with no one to turn to, and I admired his vulnerability.

As the production moved eastward, it became apparent that Gene and I were worlds apart. He was ten years older than me, quite humorous, an excellent performer, and a nice person. However, this does not always imply that you can create harmony together. We were not fighting at all. There was just some uneasiness between us. I will never understand why. Nobody gets along with everyone. Typically, actors and actresses maintain a political distance while working together, and then they separate. Every once in a while, we meet someone with whom we can connect. On The Godfather, a number of guys took me under their wing and helped me feel comfortable. I had a lifetime of acting experience, so I didn't need somebody to instruct me how to do it. To be honest, I didn't need help. Gene was a bit reserved, and we didn't really connect except in our duties. We worked. I guess Gene thought I was immature because I was so wild. And I think he might have been right.

I got along great with Gene Hackman's younger brother, Richard, who played a minor role in the picture. We were a couple of men who liked drinking and partying. The two of us went out late at night, and I'd arrive on set the next morning after only two hours of sleep. My face would be flabby and swollen from all the drinking, resembling one of those giant beach balls thrown about in Central Park.

After Scarecrow, I was itching to get back onstage. I appealed to my buddy David Wheeler, who directed the Theatre Company of Boston and had always wanted me to portray Richard III. So I went to Boston for that trip, and it turned out to be one of the most fulfilling experiences I've had since The Indian Wants the Bronx. Richard III is one of those iconic parts that has elevated the careers of actors such as Edmund Kean, John Barrymore, and Laurence Olivier. It would be my first Shakespeare play in front of a live audience, and the continuation of my trip to learn more about the character.

Richard III and I met at the Actors Studio. When I was still an unknown, I tried everything at the Actors Studio that the commercial world would never cast me in. I did musicals there, including Hamlet and Richard, with Francesca De Sapio as my Lady Anne. This new Richard arrived six or seven years after I completed it at the Actors Studio, when my life was in a different place. David Wheeler was a superb director with an excellent reputation and a man I adored, and our relationship was one of the most crucial in terms of my career. During a cold winter in Boston, we immersed ourselves in the world of Shakespeare and Richard III. It was a fascinating rehearsal session, filled with experiments and improvisations. Charlie came up to assist me practice on the role, and his wife, Penny, was there as Lady Anne.

It was also a period when I recalled my romance with Tuesday Weld. We really liked each other. We would simply sit at bars and drink Brandy Alexanders. I brought her to Boston with me. I had issues with that. And I did something I now regret. It never fails to have an impact. I just assumed that living together and performing in a play would strain our relationship. I figured that would be too much for me.

Unfortunately, three weeks of rehearsal were insufficient, and I feel unwell with a high fever. Charlie was at the foot of my bed, reviewing the lines with me. Charlie had attended one of the rehearsals and was quite excited about the progress we were making.

If we had done the play in the 1960s, in a dilapidated theater in Greenwich Village, I suppose it would have worked. However, the Loeb Drama Center in Cambridge was a significant advance. We had no actual set. There were a bunch of iron bars on some sculptures that meant nothing. I didn't comprehend it, and I was still trying to find out where I was headed with my performance.

Every night, I'd be in the church rectory getting ready to go. My state of mind was nearly insane. My career in New York was going off, and The Godfather was exploding, but I was up here in Boston, performing Richard for the second time, trying to move on from my Loeb experience. I had no idea, but alcoholism was creeping up on me, and I was struggling as normal with my romantic relationship. My overall thinking was, "Where is all of this going?" I was in chaos, but also emancipated. I transferred that wildness to Richard, who is close to that level himself. Without all of this going on, the character may not have been as available to me.

I had this Harvard intern who was assigned to be my assistant and work beside me. She was a stocky small Italian girl who, I imagined, could have easily scooped me up and hurled me on stage. We devised a game that began with my putting her on and evolved into a pre show ritual.

When we first started performing the play there, I was getting five or six curtain calls per night—each time I would take my bows, stand in the wings, and then return to the stage to bow again—and not because I was so lovely. It was because the audience had an experience watching the production. It had them. It worked because we had the aura of the cathedral; the austerity of the setting brought it to life. And it never worked again.

Six years later, I returned to Broadway to play Richard III again. And of course, we were no longer in that church. We had no vision or concept. We were doing it in a proscenium theater with that old schlub set from the Loeb. The play was not taking place. I tried to repeat myself, but it had been a while, and I was doing everything incorrectly. The reviews said—and I don't read reviews, but they always respond—"Pacino sets Shakespeare back 50 years in this country." I was wondering why they didn't mention a hundred years.

After a concert one night, I returned to my dressing room. I was fatigued. After three hours of playing Richard on that stage, I believed I deserved to sit there, bone-eyed and out of it, in my small recliner. When I looked up, there was Jacqueline Kennedy Onassis, who had come backstage with a young woman, whom I believe was her daughter, Caroline, to see me. She was so lovely and attractive, exuding class. And, as I collapsed in my chair, I extended my hand for her to kiss.

As we were preparing to launch Richard III at the Church of the Covenant in Boston, I received word that I had been nominated for an Academy Award for my performance in The Godfather. It was my first, and it seemed possible that it would be the only one I ever received. A few weeks ago, I learned that I had won the National Board of Review's Best Supporting Actor award. That felt like a major event, but I never understood why they didn't also award Best Actor to Brando. They went with Peter O'Toole instead, and while I adore Peter O'Toole, let's be honest: Marlon Brando in The Godfather changed the game.

As we were preparing to launch Richard III at the Church of the Covenant in Boston, I received word that I had been nominated for an Academy Award for my performance in The Godfather. It was my first, and it seemed possible that it would be the only one I ever received. A few weeks ago, I learned that I had won the National Board of Review's Best Supporting Actor award. That felt like a major event, but I never understood why they didn't also award Best Actor to Brando. They went with Peter O'Toole instead, and while I adore Peter O'Toole, let's be honest: Marlon Brando in The

Godfather changed the game.

I only recently discovered that the industry believed I snubbed the Oscars—that I did not attend the ceremony because I was nominated for The Godfather as a supporting actor rather than a leading man. That I felt slighted because I believed I deserved to be nominated in the same category as Marlon. It explains a lot of the disconnect I felt when I traveled to Hollywood to visit and work. It was horrifying to learn it now, after missing all of these opportunities to refute it and without even realizing what people thought of me.

These are the types of situations that can have an impact on your life in Hollywood. It causes a domino effect. People in my industry have a vested interest in the talent they represent—they might have argued that I was equivalent to Brando to raise the volume and boost that image. If I hired a private investigator to find out where this fictional story arose, that would be an option, but I still don't know how it happened. Assumptions spread, and those assumptions become opinions, which turn into stone that cannot be penetrated or changed. That's a mouthful, but I believe that's what happens the majority of the time in our world. Fabrications and rumors become facts. We're pitiful little lambs who've lost our path.

At the time, I was completely unaware of the full tale of Frank Serpico and the Knapp Commission. Serpico was one of the first cops to speak out about the corruption he witnessed and chip away at that citadel; it's impossible to make a dent in it, but he tried. I simply wasn't aware of that. Marty Bregman wanted me to play Serpico in a movie he was making about him. If I did it, Bregman would serve as both my manager and the film's producer. Sure, there is a conflict of interest. Someone is being paid to produce it, and he is receiving a percentage from you. However, I believed that the arrangement's positive aspects compensated. Because Marty recognized me. He was my partner. He was someone I felt confident I could chat to. And he'd listen.

Peter Maas wrote a biography of Serpico, and I was shown a film screenplay based on his book. Let me tell you, it went like this: "He does this." Then he does it. Then he goes there. Then he heads there. Like the novel I'm now writing. You read it and respond, "Yes?" It's like saying, "Hamlet returns home." Then he sees his dad. Then he visits his mother. Okay, good. So I wasn't interested. I needed more than that.

But then I met Frank Serpico at Bregman's office. Bregman had set it up. I only knew Frank once. I replied, "I can play him." I have to play him. I saw it in his eyes and decided I wanted to be that. I'm frequently given genuine individuals, and I decline them. I did not want to be them. Not because they are terrible or good. I just didn't feel a connection to them.

Waldo Salt and Norman Wexler collaborated to write an excellent script, which was subsequently directed by John Avildsen. He had directed some excellent films up to that point and would go on to direct Rocky. He was alright with me. I was beginning to read other performers alongside him, serving as a type of stage manager at auditions. Then one day, Avildsen disappeared. He'd been fired. That is how Marty Bregman accomplished it. I sat there, thinking, "What the fuck?" I had no idea why he fired this person; we hadn't even begun rehearsals. Avildsen has just recently begun to discuss his plans for the film. I was so immersed in the process of discovering the Serpico persona for myself, deciding how I'd play him, and growing a beard that it became my entire world. I had no idea what else was going on during the film's production. I had no idea how much money I was making; Marty would pay me $200 per week for taxicabs, and that was plenty for me.

When I was prepping for Serpico, I went on a ride with a group of cops to observe how they did it. My squad was called in to look into a probable heist in process in a tenement block. They all hurried up the stairs, pistols drawn, and that was as far as I got. Because they had no idea what to expect when they arrived at the door. I told myself that was the first and last time I would do that.

I didn't have to, actually. I had the genuine Frank Serpico as a reference, and he was incredibly educated and helpful. During the summer, when we were filming the picture, I was riding in a taxi to a location and dressed as Serpico. We wound up behind a truck that began to emit massive amounts of pollution. As if the atmosphere wasn't already contaminated enough. Then I recognized what I was doing.

I was still dating Tuesday Weld when I began work on Serpico. Every morning, I would get up and go to work in a specific area. Then at night, I went out drinking with her. I'd already been filming for a few weeks and understood how much effort would be expected of me. That put pressure on the relationship, and I knew we couldn't continue much longer. We were young enough, and we hadn't been together long enough, so I guess I saw the handwriting on the wall, so to speak, that now was the time for us to split up. I couldn't be in this film while being with someone.

I could see a pattern emerging in me, an inherent sense that a job is work, and romance and life come second. I've heard a lot about folks who are extremely involved and focused on their work. They lose vital relationships due to their commitment to their profession and the need to provide their all. I can joyfully state that I am no longer like that, but at the time, I was already coming to that conclusion about myself.

I sought sanctuary in my work on Serpico. The nicest part of filmmaking is the toast before you begin shooting. You're a happy group, all chatting about how fortunate you are to be doing what you do. We held Serpico at Dino De Laurentiis' home, which had a fantastic apartment at the top of a building on Central Park South. It had floor to ceiling windows. You could see China from his location.

I felt like I had arrived. Peter Maas was present. We had Waldo Salt, Norman Wexler, Sidney Lumet, and Marty Bregman. There is no woman in sight. The six of us appeared like small Lego people standing in the midst of all this wealth.

I was assigned a driver who would pick me up every day, drive me to where we were filming, and bring me home at night. He was an older man, and I truly loved him, but he despised his job. He despised driving, loathed being trapped in traffic, and was often irritated. I used to tease him just to see if I could provoke a reaction from him. He pulled up in front of the restaurant and got out, leaving the key in the ignition and the engine running. As soon as he did, I hopped into the front seat and took off in the automobile. But I just drove around the corner to spy on him as he exited the restaurant, watching his mute confusion as he tried to figure out if his car and the star of the film had been taken.

When Serpico finished filming, I went out drinking with Charlie at a swanky bar on Madison Avenue, just across the corner from where I was staying at the time. Charlie and I were ossified, and I met this woman who was also a bit loaded. She was a tall girl dressed in a wild black dress and six-inch heels, as was customary for the time. Charlie went home, and I led her up to my apartment, where I collapsed on my bed, totally dressed. So did she, even with her six-inch heels. The two of us accomplished nothing. I went across town to a screening room where they were preparing to show the first rough cut of Serpico and stepped in with this female dressed in black and wearing six-inch heels. And they were all there: Sidney Lumet, Dino De Laurentiis, and Dede Allen, the legendary film editor who worked on The Hustler and Bonnie and Clyde. Marty Bregman was present, and he was steaming. He had made many films and seen considerably worse than this. The lights went off, the film began, and I asked this girl how she felt about it. I don't remember her specific remarks, but her demeanor was one of general disregard.

Serpico turned out fairly well. It earned me my second Oscar nomination, and Marty Bregman had done so much for me and the picture that I couldn't miss the event. However, I was still afraid. I boarded the plane with Marty, Charlie, and Diane Keaton, with whom I was working on The Godfather: Part II at the time. Of course, I got stoned.

I was seated with Diane to my right, making minor show-related jokes, and she laughed. But then the jokes got a little old, and I'm taking Valiums and waiting for something. To my left was Jeff Bridges. I could still tell the time at that moment. I looked at my watch and thought, "This is crazy." They haven't won the Best Actor award. So I turned to Jeff, whom I would later get to know as one of the most remarkable people and actors. I was just faintly aware when it came time to reveal my category. I am blotto. I'm in such a bad situation that I need to go somewhere and sit quietly while someone administers shock treatments. I thought, "This cannot be happening." I can't win in this room. I've been nominated against Robert Redford, Jack Nicholson, Marlon Brando, and Jack Lemmon. I didn't give a speech since I knew I wouldn't win. I was more optimistic than anything.

It's likely they will announce my name. They're vengeful, these Academy members. They'll probably give you the prize solely to fuck with you. Then I began to shiver. I was jacked up on Valium and terrified of everything. They announced the nominees' names. I just smiled and screamed with happiness. If someone saw me on television, they probably wouldn't know. They just observed my lifeless expression, but the sentiments inside were genuine. It's a real relief.

Chapter 6: The Business We've Chosen

Mario Puzo was someone I could always rely on to tell me the truth. He asked me to meet him one night at the Ginger Man. It was to give me an early look at the script he was working on for The Godfather: Part II. He passed me a copy across our table so that I could read it at my leisure as I pondered the weighty question of whether I wanted to return to the role of Michael Corleone and all the responsibilities that entailed. Before I began, he wanted me to know one particular thing.

Nothing about it reminded me of The Godfather. Francis did not want to be involved. He had turned it down, but they were still following him. They wanted me too, because my character was still alive at the end of the first film. They continued coming to me with pricing, and they kept going up. First, $100,000. Then $200,000. Then they raised it to $600,000. That was real money back then. But I did not enjoy the script. Mario was a great writer and he was going to succeed. But they asked me to commit to something that didn't exist.

The film's producer summoned me to his New York office. He placed a large bottle of Scotch on the table, and I thought, Wow, he is going to get me high. We liked one other a lot, so I began talking to him as he poured me a drink. It was completely out of my league. It was an abstraction. And it made absolutely no difference. So Charlie and I flew to San Francisco, booked a room at the Fairmont Hotel, and worked back and forth. We'd talk to Francis, and he'd write and return it to us. I have no idea how to write a script. I merely knew the furniture was already there, but you'd need moving workers to transport everything into the house. That is what Charlie and I were. The story contained missing links.

Michael lacked the dimensions of his father, Vito, whose character had been shaped by his time in the old country and the hardships of poverty, pulling himself up by his bootstraps. Michael could navigate his family's violent domain with ease, despite the fact that he was forced to do so. That is the individual we see in the first Godfather picture, learning about his gift, if you will.

Part II features a different Michael. By the end of Part II, Michael has become nearly immobile. But, to get him there, I had to return to where I had left Michael at the end of the first film, when he had become that suddenly scary figure who could have other guys lining up only to kiss his ring. The image he creates at the end of the first Godfather is simple: who is that guy? I do not want to go near him. At least that's what I was attempting to do: represent him as enigmatic and deadly. The danger for me was in the task ahead: returning to where Michael had left off at the end of the previous excursion and pushing myself to figure out where I would take him next.

One of Francis and Mario's clever innovations for Part II was a new competitor for Michael, Hyman Roth, a veteran mobster and old accomplice of his father's, who seems to him as an ally and partner. See, it's always the ones you least expect that you have to be wary of, at least in that line of employment. Hyman Roth was modeled after Meyer Lansky and was intended to be as brilliant, if not brighter, than Michael. Francis had wanted Elia Kazan to play him, but Kazan declined, and while I read with some other interesting candidates, like Samuel Fuller, the filmmaker and screenwriter, no one seemed to meet the criteria.

Francis still needed convincing, so I took him to a large party for the Actors Studio. It was in a ballroom, and the speakers were all seated on a dais. When it was Lee's turn to address the crowd, we sat and listened to him, and he talked with great wit and comedy. He had been a renowned tutor to Marilyn Monroe and Dustin Hoffman, but he could be as amusing as Groucho Marx when he wanted to. So Francis was won over and gave him the position, and I thought that would be fantastic—now Lee and I would be working together, and

I'd get to know him better.

I appeared to have met and accumulated these types of people throughout my life, surrogates for the father I never had. Now I had three people in the mix: Charlie, my manager Marty Bregman, and Lee Strasberg. I'm not sure if they felt possessive over me, but I have to believe they did. They occupied distinct lanes. Marty was concerned with my career advancement, success, and fame, and all the associated benefits. Charlie was more concerned with the reality of my profession and the person it made me. I believe Charlie and Marty maintained a certain diplomatic distance from one another. Charlie appreciated and respected Marty, recognizing his strength and intelligence. Marty recognized Charlie's importance to my acting development and spiritual well-being. I'm sure they each had their own interpretation of the other, and they were kind enough not to express it in front of me.

Lee's entry into that formula did not necessarily complicate matters further. Lee was a completely different type of character. Lee was always very nutritious for me, and I appreciated his company. I was fascinated in him, as I am in all persons with such intellectual breadth and unpredictability in their perspectives. Lee's expressions were brief and straightforward. He kept a home on Fire Island, where he would spend the summer with his family. And, as the tale goes, they all went swimming on a hot day, except for Lee, who sat and observed the others.

When Francis and I worked on The Godfather, we were younger and greener, which excused many of our faults and occasional disagreements. Part II was different. When Francis agreed to direct it as well, I realized how much of the responsibility for its success rested on his shoulders. We had a terrible time with Part II, but I still admired him, and we wanted to do everything we could to work together.

When we first began filming at Lake Tahoe, we focused on images from Michael's son's Communion party. We were out in the cold one night, sitting at a table with Mike Gazzo, who was amazing as Frank Pentangeli. It's so chilly that we're putting ice in our lips to prevent smoke from coming out when we speak. They had finished shooting my side of a party scene and were now filming Mike Gazzo. People at the scene began to leave for the night, and plans were made to begin disassembling the equipment. We're all outside in the bitter cold.

Francis gritted his teeth somewhat when I told him this. I gritted my teeth because I had to bring it up. It meant that everyone had to return to their positions in the scene, all of the equipment that they had begun to disassemble had to be reassembled, and further takes had to be filmed. It was truly not my place to request any of this. But Francis understood that indicated I was immersed in my role and thinking things through from the character's point of view. Will Michael Corleone react to such behavior at a table? Of course. Francis did it because he knew what was required. That is what it means to work together.

While we were filming in Tahoe, I was assigned a bodyguard. He was exceedingly short and slender as a wire, the type of person we used to nickname a wolverine. He was a genuine Westerner whose ancestors had to have lived long before the Civil War. He wore a sheriff's badge, though I don't believe he had ever been a sheriff, and he carried a half-sized revolver at his side. He finished his look with a cowboy hat. Because it could spark a minor dispute. Barroom brawl was always a possibility in the places we visited. We did get into some serious fights a few times, but we always tried to avoid them.

I used music in the film on occasion, maybe for a few scenes, to help me reconnect with Michael. I'd walk into a dressing room, put on headphones, and blast Stravinsky, Beethoven, or Mozart at full volume. I'd just saturate my brain with stuff, then emerge to play in a scenario. It was a method I devised to teach myself where my brain should go—where my entire spirit should go—so that I might have a sense of recollection of it when I recorded the scene. I didn't have to listen to the music while the cameras were rolling; I could simply go to that location in my brain and it would be there. I've seen actors do this with animals, studying the spirit of a bulldog or a swan and attempting to locate an element of it in themselves. This was just an intuition I had about music, so I didn't have to knock on tables or jump up and down, and it appeared to work well. It was not a method I utilized in the first Godfather or any other roles I played. But that was just what I needed for Michael now. I never reveal these kinds of secrets, yet others want to know them.

Diane and I were always fond of each other and liked spending time together. We met because of The Godfather, but something had changed in Part II, and I couldn't reestablish that connection with her. I was still reeling from the pain of breaking up with Tuesday, whom I adored, still yearning and complaining about her, and still dealing with the fallout. I was heavily into drink and drugs, getting high and losing myself in a cloud. I preferred the state of semi consciousness. Charlie spent a few days with me in Tahoe, but once he went, I was alone. I was suffering through something less serious than depression, yet a sense of melancholy had crept over me.

Most likely, it was also due to the role I was portraying. I assumed I was participating in the role. But I was in a Michael Corleone trance, and the role took a lot out of me. Fortunately, I understood Michael because I portrayed him in the first Godfather. But in Part II, I encountered a different version of this character—on the same spectrum, but with distinct challenges, complexities, and dimensions. He traveled to certain regions within himself, and getting myself there required some work. I immersed myself in this character, let go of the reins and control, and decided I'd simply go with it. I felt it helpful to see the young Michael at the end of Part II, early in his life and younger than he was in Part 1. You got a feeling of his core and personality, which allowed him to absorb and inhabit the life he was in. His father knew he could do it. That is why Michael was chosen.

The shoot in Santo Domingo, the Dominican Republic's capital, which was also serving as Havana toward the end of 1958, was not particularly enjoyable. In the film, Hyman Roth and the other heads of the organized crime families have gathered to cut Cuba up for themselves, but Michael is concerned because he recently witnessed a revolutionary blow himself up in the streets, leaving him wondering if the Cuba they want will still exist. And before long, the government is ousted, and Michael and his colleagues are forced to flee—every man for himself. Michael must also confront the awful knowledge that his brother Fredo played a role in the attempted murder of him and his entire family in Tahoe.

I felt isolated. I'm not sure why, but the set didn't feel right, and the days seemed endless. It may take up to four days to shoot a scene since they had to wait hours for the lighting to be perfect. I was just thirty-four years old, but it was proving difficult. Meanwhile, I'm carrying the emotions of a man who discovered that his own brother attempted to have him assassinated. It was heavy. As an actor, I should be used to this. I frequently play characters who are confronted with difficult situations. I have a role, and I fulfill it. I've since learned how to handle the craft more effectively, so the role no longer drains me as much. But Michael Corleone was a difficult man to live with. Finding peace in your soul was difficult.

Then there's the scene where the brothers discover each other on the floor of the New Year's Eve celebration, and Michael grabs Fredo and kisses him, whispering to him that he knows he's betrayed him. He kisses his own brother on the lips, the kiss of death. That was in the script and was well directed and executed. Sometimes you think to yourself, "Boy, I hope they caught that on camera," and you're relieved when they do. It reminded me of a line from a movie where John Barrymore had to kill his brother, Lionel.

But when we weren't shooting, I found myself lonely and in need of companionship. John Cazale and I were lifelong acquaintances, but he had brought his girlfriend. I would go into the pool with Lee Strasberg's children and swim and play with them, but they were quite small at the time and were primarily with their mother and father. I was drinking, but not to the point where it affected my work. I've never done that. But a cloud had rolled over me.

My social gene hadn't fully evolved yet. I was still avoiding stardom and all that came with it. I wasn't always a miserable sack. We were in Santo Domingo when I received my Oscar nomination for Serpico. I organized a party to celebrate, inviting the entire crew and everyone in attendance. So I was thrilled at that point.

There was a definite vibe in and around The Godfather: Part II. I was portraying a powerful deity, and Francis was at the pinnacle of his filmmaking and show business abilities. Because of The Godfather, we suddenly had positions in the world, power, and recognition, and we were both in the Dominican Republic, separated from the lives and people we knew back home. We all agreed on the writing, Michael's interpretation, and how the character was developing.

There was some tension between us at times. Perhaps it was simply a lack of communication and familiarity, or it could be the result of the six days and nights we spent working on the script with Charlie. I realized how much it mattered to Francis that I portray Michael, even more than it did to me. He saw me in the role, offered me an incredible opportunity, and fought for me. Nonetheless, we were worlds apart. I actually contacted him lately and asked him about our time together shooting The Godfather: Part II. He couldn't remember it and couldn't say. But I remember it as a time when we were relatively apart from one another, and I'm glad it didn't continue long. Francis and I shared similar perspectives on many issues, and I genuinely admire him. He has a tremendous intellect and epic talent, and I like hearing his perspectives on any topic. He had created one fantastic film, and now we were attempting to complete a second.

Chapter 7: Maximum Velocity

I was staring at the purple curtain in my opulent hotel room in London. I watched as a mouse rushed up the fabric, only to be ambushed by a bat that appeared out of nowhere. I wasn't sure if what I was witnessing was genuine, a hallucination, or a flashback to the movie The Lost Weekend, which my mother had taken me to when I was five years old. I was whirling out.

I threw my shaky glance into the distance and saw Charlie sitting at the opposite end of a long table, each of us holding a large bottle of strong liquor by our sides. I believed I could see my future: getting so intoxicated that I began to see things that did not exist. I was at risk of developing delirium tremens, sometimes known as the d.t.s. Back in my twenties, while recovering from surgery in a New York hospital, they gave me morphine, and when I woke up, I imagined I was flying through the air above Central Park. Now I was in London, and as I stared out from a sixth-floor luxury room overlooking St. James's Park, I wondered whether a similar feeling might wash over me and carry me right out that window.

Frank Pierson had written a firecracker of a story about a failed bank heist that escalated into a hostage situation in Brooklyn a few summers ago. Marty Bregman had worked hard to get several of the actual participants in the theft to sell their rights to the story. Bregman had Pierson write the screenplay and Sidney Lumet, our golden boy from Serpico, was set to helm it. Naturally, he wanted me to be the star. Naturally, I turned it down.

Lumet offered us three weeks to practice Dog Day Afternoon, which allowed me to develop my character, Sonny Wortzik. Then I filmed the first day on film. For some reason, I went to the rushes afterward to see the tape, which is not something I would normally do. But something made me watch it. When I looked around, I realized I wasn't playing anybody. I do not have a character. I need to be a person here because I do not see anyone.

I had a small flat on Sixty-Eighth and Madison in a lovely Upper East Side area. The neighborhood was calm, wholesome, and rich, and the building was quite private, which I appreciated. There were no doormen and no lobby through which I had to interact with others. Candice Bergen had previously occupied the apartment, but it was now mine. The rent was reasonable, and there were just three rooms: a tiny bedroom, a living room with a couch and a fireplace, and a very small kitchen with a window that reminded me of the one where my grandmother used to hang out while she washed her clothes. The space suited me. It kept me safe from the city's turmoil, except for a lady I heard screaming every other night. She was in the midst of something horrible. It had the potential to drive a person away, but I persisted.

The night before the reshoot for Dog Day Afternoon, I found myself alone in the flat with half a gallon of white wine. I spent about half of the night pacing the floor, sipping wine, and deciding which direction I wanted to take with the film's primary character. I felt like I was attempting to create a sonata or write a short tale. In my seclusion, I was attempting to find a place, a route, that would motivate the character and allow for some spontaneity. I needed to come up with something quick.

Charlie was the one who suggested we cast John Cazale as my accomplice in crime. Even though Sidney Lumet preferred someone younger, Charlie was spot on—John was an amazing pillar of that film, and the dynamic between our characters was a perfect reversal of how we interacted in the Godfather films. Anyone who expected a rerun of Michael and Fredo Corleone was surprised.

When the shoot was finished, the persona I had played simply flew out of me. I'd been possessed, and suddenly it was gone. Even Sidney told me that he saw it go like a spirit. When we returned later to reshoot a few items, the spirit had not returned. We did the reshoots, and I got through them. Some of these moments did not live up to my expectations, but I had seen enough of the film to get by. I doubt any viewers could tell which parts were reshoots, because when I look at the film, I can't tell. Sometimes we have images of ourselves that are completely off-center.

Perhaps it was unusual at the time of Dog Day Afternoon to have a gay or queer main character in a Hollywood film who was portrayed as heroic or deserving of an audience's affection—even if he did rob banks. But you must understand that I take none of this into consideration. I am an actress who plays a character in a film. I'm performing the role because I believe I can offer something to it. As far as I was concerned, Dog Day Afternoon was simply cool, a continuation of the job I'd done my entire life. It was unavoidable that an audience would form opinions about me based on the decisions I made, and the slings and arrows would continue to fly regardless. I try to avoid difficult topics, yet I end up becoming involved in them anyhow. If individuals believe I helped to progress a specific issue of representation, that's fine. If there is credit or blame to be shared, I don't feel entitled to any of it. All I know is that my responsibility is to express as much humanity as possible.

The most powerful scene in the entire film was a spontaneous fabrication. He was referring to an upstate New York jail where a riot had broken out a few months before and was ruthlessly suppressed by the governor, prison staff, and police. So I went outside and started talking to the audience. And I thought, "That's what a film can be." Go out and do it. Something may happen. That's what Burtt Harris knew. And of course, we went with it, and here it is. It's Attica. Congratulations, Burtt Harris!

Norman Ornellas was one of my best pals in the performing world. He had been with me for many career achievements, and I felt I knew him well. But I first met his father in a hospital when Norman was dying from cancer. Norman was thirty-five, too young to be on the edge of dying. Norman was a brilliant Actors Studio performer who had served time in prison and had a wild, gritty edge. But he was really educated and gifted, and I adored him. He had appeared in Serpico, Richard III, and The Resistible Rise of Arturo Ui, and he had recently made his Broadway debut in a play directed by Joe Papp. Norman began treatments after receiving his diagnosis; he had been doing so for a few weeks when we met for lunch at the Ginger Man and told me what was going on.

Maybe it looked like an odd request from his poor father, but it wasn't any more ridiculous than some of the things I'd attempted to do to help Norman as he became increasingly ill. I became desperate in my own hunt for answers, turning to psychic mediums and persons who performed séances, quack physicians who offered ludicrous cure-alls, and pretty much any approach that claimed to heal him of his sickness. Whatever it is, you ask yourself, "Why not give it a try?" Finally, you realize that everything is beyond our control.

Norman, John Cazale, and I had been talking about founding a theater together. Joe Papp was involved, and we were talking with him about building a national theater in America that would be financed by the government, similar to what they have in England, and would include other actresses such as Meryl Streep, whom John was dating. However, because the film industry is concentrated on the West Coast, it has proven difficult to establish a national theater in New York. You can establish a national theatre in London because all of the actors live there. But in America, all of the performers are spread out between New York and Los Angeles, which is three thousand miles away from where we planned to shoot in New York. I, too, was living in a dream world since I was about to become a star. I thought, "I can't get stuck doing only theater when I know I have another life ahead of me."

I was astonished to learn that John Cazale never visited Norman in the hospital. I'm not sure if John realized he had cancer yet. John was a sensitive person who appreciated the role of actors as prophets and seers. I believe he did not want the prophecy of what could happen to him. I knew John didn't want to have children, and perhaps that was why.

When John received his own cancer diagnosis and began telling others about it, I would occasionally accompany him to his doctor's office for his treatments. He was a fantastic artist and confidant, and I wanted to work with him all the time.

Dog Day Afternoon was a triumph. I was on a roll, continuing my unusual run of pictures that included The Godfather, Serpico, and The Godfather: Part II. Another critical success. Another box office success. Another Oscar nomination I did not attend. (Everyone said I wouldn't stand a chance against Jack Nicholson in One Flew Over the Cuckoo's Nest, and trust me, I was psychologically incapable of going, whether Jack was a sure thing.)

You're pretty much on your own in dealing with this. There aren't many people around you who can tell you, here's how you deal with it, here's how you grapple with it—this new intensity of a transformed life, one that leads to terrible solitude and a peculiar manner of being cut off from the rest of the world. It remains, as far as I can tell, an unanswered question. And how I dealt with that was to use drugs and drink. I was not living the high life. My approach to coping was more low-key and secretive. I tried going to the theater again. I returned to the Actors Studio and tried several things. But I was experiencing extreme anxiousness. Nerves. And I had many alcohol problems. And it all happened with me alone in a modest flat.

Charlie had finally given up drinking because he realized he was an alcoholic. He and I were always going somewhere. I believe Bregman looked at us and thought, "That's what they do." As I already stated, I rarely drank in front of Bregman. He had no idea I had an issue with it. I had no idea I had an issue with it. But Charlie was aware, and he understood that I was unaware. I thought I was okay. I didn't drink at work—that was my main thing. Work was always first. It gave me identity and peace, making me feel more connected to who I am.

I went to Alcoholics Anonymous for a while. I had a taste of it, but it didn't feel anonymous to me. I also did not relate personally to that setting, but I realize it's worth it, and the service it provides to individuals in need is amazing. I simply felt out of place there, so I walked on. Increasing my involvement in one-on-one therapy proved beneficial. It helped me keep going and quit drinking. It almost feels like it's required in my position. C'mon, buddy, you need to shrink your skull. Because your head grows so large, you must reduce it. You need to go to a guy who will tell you everything you already know about yourself and pay you attention for an hour. Which we all enjoy. We all need some care.

I first saw a psychiatrist in Boston before moving to New York to find a boyfriend. I fell in love with the process and eventually found myself in therapy five days a week at specific times. If you're thinking about going to therapy, I highly recommend it. Maybe you don't need it five times a week, but try it. There is an old story. A woman sees a therapist for years. It's her final appointment because she believes she's reached a high point in her life and is ready to move on. She would like to applaud her therapist and say farewell. That is also an interpretation of therapy. You need to talk and let it all out. Before I went to therapy, I used to sit in the bathtub alone and chat about stuff. I kept my thoughts to myself.

It's an odd bond that you form when you meet a decent doctor who you believe is committed to you. Then they take a huge amount of time off, and you don't see them for the entire summer. I had one of those situations where I couldn't find my doctor. If I could have avoided the tsuris, I could have saved myself around twenty years. It's a good idea to know where your psychiatrist is so you can contact them if you're in trouble. They, too, need to rest. I used to have recurring dreams about going to my psychiatrist's office but not being able to find him. He is in the building, but he is unavailable. I'm at the door, but there's no buzzer to alert him to my presence, and there's no means for him to let me in. That was my dream. I now have that sensation about my agent.

I gradually weaned myself off of booze. My first film following that was Bobby Deerfield, which I consider to be one of my most revealing performances. I was attempting to understand someone who was alone and afraid of death, yet who faced it every day. Bobby's life goal is to drive Formula One race cars quicker than anybody else, a career in which every mistake might be catastrophic. He is pursued by loving admirers but disillusioned with his celebrity, and he has already abandoned his family and his previous life when a race accident kills one driver and paralyzes another. The whole ordeal leaves him in a walking, talking coma.

While visiting the surviving driver in the hospital, Bobby encounters a woman who has been diagnosed with a deadly sickness. She's attempting to feel life in some manner, to experience it and surrender herself to it. She isn't impressed by his work or aware of his popularity, and despite the fact that her fate will be tragic, and because of her youth, she is attempting to overcome whatever occurs to a young person when they are told they won't live long. Bobby makes contact with something, and it transforms him.

There was certainly nothing like driving that race car. You haven't lived until you've witnessed one of those cars turn a corner at 170 mph. It doesn't seem feasible, but it does. I had the opportunity to meet and learn from two of the top drivers of the time, Clay Regazzoni and Jackie Stewart, at Le Mans. It's really difficult to get behind the wheel and do what they do, let alone capture it on film.

No way. They have fifteen gears in that device. I'm lucky I went 20 mph. I was frightened I'd go off a cliff. But I met the guys and saw what they did. They had a team of skilled drivers who would record all the challenging racing moments, which would then be included in the film. Thank god for inserts.

The studios and Sydney Pollack sought a few people to play the film's love interests. I met a couple actresses who appeared okay to me. But then they went with Marthe Keller, a fantastic actress who had previously appeared in Marathon Man and Black Sunday. Marthe was Swiss and quite refined; she had studied at Berlin's famous theaters and spoke English with a faint accent. She was completely foreign to me. But I had fallen in love with her. And somehow, she fell in love with me.

Not right away. I was not interested in her. Neither does she in me. She never showed me any signs. I always assumed she was a little sad that Redford did not make the film. That made complete sense to me. But I was hurt when I met her, and it's likely that a part of her was drawn to the Bobby Deerfield in me. I'd never met anyone like her. And she had definitely never met anyone like me. She was a tall, elegant, polished European woman. And I was this South Bronx person who was self-taught and perhaps a touch unrefined in her eyes. And sometimes, that is what defines a relationship.

Charlie Bluhdorn, the wild and crazy genius who controlled Paramount Pictures, became a friend of mine due to The Godfather's success. I met him at one of the more upscale New York parties I'd been invited to with Marthe—the type of gathering where you may wind up shaking hands with everyone from Andy Warhol to Henry Kissinger. Charlie Bluhdorn spotted Marthe and me at this party, took one look at us, and invented the nickname "the Odd Couple," which perfectly describes us.

From Bobby Deerfield on, I was done drinking. I was completely off, and every subsequent interaction was tainted with a sense of distance and timidity. This appeared to be my demeanor when I broke off the alcohol, which had been my prescription. After that, it felt like I was always on edge. I consider myself fortunate to have overcome that obstacle, and Marthe was a huge help in getting me over it. There was much affection there. Our connection has evolved over the years, primarily as friends, but I am grateful to her.

I am not sure what the reviews stated about Bobby Deerfield, but I am sure they were awful. You can always tell when you make a film. I received a note from a friend shortly after it was published, expressing her displeasure with the hostility directed at me. I hadn't read any of it, but I now knew. She meant well, but I would have rather not heard that. So I had a poor opinion of the film.

When it launched in New York, the studios threw a massive party at Tavern on the Green. I didn't even attend it. It gave me many problems. I knew if I went, I wouldn't enjoy it. This wasn't my thing, especially because I believed the film didn't work. The studios actually gave me my own sports car, an Alfa Romeo, as a gift. But it had a manual transmission, and I didn't know how to use it. Then Bobby Deerfield failed so miserably that they had to return the automobile.

Making films without drinking wasn't the only thing that drew me back into the world, but it was a start. Right after, I began visiting colleges in Los Angeles, the Bronx, and throughout the country. I did refuse cash for these presentations; I did it as a donation to these schools, and I would have paid them because it was therapeutic and beneficial for me to get out there and start speaking. I would read to the students and perform poetry or roles from my plays. I was no longer self-isolating. We'd have question-and-answer sessions afterward, and I'd interact with the crowd.

I informed the woman who asked the inquiry that I had difficulty accepting media attention. I hadn't realized that the media is truly serving the public—they're showing the audience what they want to see, and the audience wants to know more about the many people who act for them. Being shy, I didn't appreciate all of the media's attention, and I certainly didn't like the paparazzi meddling with my life, but I've since realized that the media and the paparazzi, well, they have to eat as well. I wasn't sure how to handle it at the moment. But now I was reconnecting with the world, which felt fantastic. It nearly felt like survival.

Going to college allowed me to rediscover my theatrical side and connect with audiences. That, I believe, inspired my next endeavor, David Rabe's excellent play The Basic Training of Pavlo Hummel. Joe Papp had staged it at the Public with several performers, and I had done it in Boston years earlier, so I recreated it on Broadway. Pavlo is about a soldier who is slain in Vietnam. It is a large production with a cast of approximately 25 or 30 individuals, and we all worked as a team. David Wheeler superbly directed us, and I won my second Tony Award that summer.

Chapter 8: Every Day Above Ground Is a Good Day

I stood in the emergency room of a Santa Monica hospital, looking like someone who had died. I was waiting to be seen by a doctor. My eyes were lifeless and dark, and my skin was wet with sweat. My clothing was tattered and blood-stained. I was ordered to keep my arms in the air because the machine gun I was holding had fused with my hand. Only hours earlier, I was on the smoke-filled set of a mansion, where the mad, coked-out Tony Montana was making his final stand. I had just fired thirty bullets from my "little friend" in a shootout with the tiny army who had arrived to take me out. With bullets flying everywhere, the scene called for me to be shot in the upper torso, which pushed me backward. Squibs inside my suit exploded with crimson dye, sending me falling to the ground. In my character's drug-induced state, I grabbed the red-hot barrel of the machine gun I'd been firing, which was laying beside me. My hand would not move—it was stuck to the barrel.

Paul Muni appeared to be capable of doing anything on screen when he played Tony Camonte in the first Scarface, which was released in 1932. When I watched Muni in that film, written by Ben Hecht and directed by Howard Hawks, I was no longer a child sitting by my mother in an old movie theater in the South Bronx. I was a grown man and a successful actor.Muni influenced me. I wanted to copy him. I wanted to be him. I told myself, "I think I can do Scarface." I believe we can remake this. It would take us a few more years to develop our version of Scarface, which was released in 1983. Oliver Stone wrote the screenplay, Brian De Palma directed it, and Marty Bregman provided the concept. It was direct and provocative, exactly like the original. It was as American as the flag. Depending on your perspective, Scarface was the most successful film I ever made. But not straight away—not even close. In fact, it was one of several films that prompted me to leave the film industry for over four years. I got hammered for it, and then I was out for the count.

Bregman had been my staunch backer, but in 1978 we had a disagreement over a film project, and I went too far. We broke up. We went our separate ways for several years. In the meantime, I started having troubles. The film's climactic scene, which likely earned me an Oscar nomination, is my character, a Baltimore defense attorney, defending a judge he knows is guilty of rape and sexual assault. Instead, he gives a barn-burning speech in front of the jury and the entire court, telling them that his own client should go straight to fucking jail. That eruption became part of the culture in ways that the film did not.

We had spent weeks making the film in Baltimore, including several days on one sequence alone. When the courtroom segment is completed, production will move to Los Angeles. After a few days of filming that court sequence, Jewison decided he was done, and it was time for us to head to Los Angeles and finish the rest of the picture. We met in a screening room on the studio lot. Norman, Stan, and I sat in the crowd and watched the scene.

Howard Hawks, one of the finest directors of all time, created an incredible work of filmmaking. The original Scarface is a crazy reflection on the excesses and failures of the Great Depression. It was full of violence, which it appeared to justify by declaring itself, in its own title cards, "an indictment of gang rule in America and of the callous indifference of the government to this constantly increasing menace to our safety and liberty." And in the middle of it all was Paul Muni, who appeared impervious to any challenge. He was like Brando in The Wild One, a person unencumbered by rules or traditions. He made me feel something. He was free.

However, Cruising sparked heated debate throughout development. We had a lot of problems filming it in the summer of 1979, with protesters appearing at our shooting locations virtually every day.

They feared it would portray LGBT people unfairly and stereotypically. I received bomb threats and had bodyguards protect me. I already don't do well in controversies, especially when you're the so-called movie star and are expected to have all the power, but you don't. I've always believed that being silent in those situations is the best course of action, because yapping only makes everything worse. You have to roll with the punches. This is the beast's nature.

However, the film was exploitative. I didn't perceive it that way while I was doing it. When I answered yes, I expected a murder-mystery thriller with an edge. However, I was not as sensitive as I could have been to the stigmatization of the LGBT community and how this media portrayed them. And when I viewed the film, I knew it was exploitative. Let's be honest: I didn't do any publicity at the time.

I never accepted the Cruising paycheck. I took the money, which was a lot, and put it in an irrevocable trust fund, which meant that once I gave it, it could not be taken back. I donated it to organizations, and with interest, it was able to last several decades. I'm not sure if it eased my conscience, but the money did some good. It was always contributed anonymously because I didn't want it to be a publicity stunt—all I wanted was one positive outcome from the entire process.

Two years later, I created the comedy Author! Author! I couldn't say no to Israel Horovitz, who authored the screenplay and also penned The Indian Wants the Bronx. Indian culture provided me with a way of life—or a career, if you will. Let's face it—it did. Author! Author! was a comedy that attempted to explore how parents raise children in broken families, how they deal with divorce, and the drama and anguish that it brings for them and their children. And I enjoyed working with the youngsters in the film.

Of course, many people believe I am or was a cocaine addict. It may surprise you to learn that I've never touched the substance. However, I've always had a lot of energy—I'm always upbeat—and Tony Montana allowed me to channel that into the persona. He also brought me a sense of liberation. He noticed an advertising message on the side of a blimp that said THE WORLD IS YOURS and believed it wholeheartedly. That is what motivated me about him, and what I learned from him.

Our Scarface was not set during the Great Depression, the era of the Bowery Boys and Clifford Odets' plays, when everything was scarce and no one seemed to have two nickels to rub together. Our Scarface was about modern-day avarice, the Reagan period, when everything was available but still out of reach. We were criticizing the concept of trickle-down economics and the current grab-everything-you-can mindset.

Marty Bregman and I had spent some time apart, which was eventually beneficial to us. He had wanted to make films independently, away from me. And when I told him about Scarface, he sprang back into action, as if nothing had happened. He immediately struck a deal with Universal for the rights to remake the film and began collecting the cast. Bregman hired our old acquaintance Sidney Lumet to direct, and David Rabe tried a script that was more closely fashioned after the original picture, but it didn't work. So Bregman commissioned Oliver Stone, now an Academy Award winner for Midnight Express, to write it.

Lumet smartly provided the notion to modernize Scarface by placing it during the Mariel boatlift and portraying Tony Montana as one of the thousands of Cuban refugees who came to America as a mocking gift from Fidel Castro. However, Bregman wanted to avoid anything like Serpico or Dog Day Afternoon, whilst Lumet intended to make the film grounded and realistic, with themes of social conscience. Bregman said we've seen it before. The two quickly were at conflict, and Bregman fired Lumet. The Don attacked again. In came De

Palma, who wanted the film to be operatic, colorful, and immensely entertaining, just as Bregman had envisioned.

Tony Montana delivers exactly what you see, and screw you. For me, his two-dimensionality is what makes him attractive. If we wanted to get inside Tony, I didn't have to go very deep. It was right there in the text. You saw it on the page. The guy, as I played him, never has any internal difficulty until he kills his best friend, Manny, after discovering his sister in his arms. That was the one time you ever saw him baffled, in self-examination, unsure of what he accomplished. That's when he enters the third dimension, albeit only for a brief time—as far as anyone can go on that much cocaine. You know there's just death after that.

I spent the summer prepping for Scarface at the Outrigger, a large condominium complex on Malibu Beach, where I immersed myself in the role of Tony and learned everything I could about him. I'm not sure, but I can almost swear a pornographic film was being made next door to me. I would occasionally hear strange noises and watch my neighbors come and leave in scanty outfits that hinted at their movie endeavors. But in my room, with a view of the Pacific Ocean, I was meeting with my costume designer, makeup artist, and hair stylist to discuss my character. How about the scar? How did he get that? Where does it go? I came up with a concept. I responded, "I want a scar that runs through his brow and into his face." It states it right away. There it is: anarchy. That's Tony Montana. All you need to do is gaze at him.

We ran into some production issues early on when we began filming in Miami that fall. There was a conservative contingent there who were concerned about how we could depict Cubans in our film— would we exploit them, be insulting, or be pro-Castro?—and they would periodically try to cause problems for us at shooting locations. When you go deep enough into these issues, you usually discover that some politicians are attempting to make a statement or that someone's wheel hasn't been greased. But eventually, I would become the biggest villain on the set.

I was grateful for my amazing relationship with Kathleen Quinlan. I first met Kathleen at a gathering at Lee Strasberg's home on Central Park West, where Lee would gather guests on Sunday nights to talk about music, theater, and the arts. Bob De Niro was with me, and at one point I saw Kathleen. She turned to look at me. I looked at her and that was it. The thunderbolt had struck me.

Kathleen turned out to have a boyfriend. Any lady with a boyfriend or husband is off limits. I just won't go there. I'm guessing it's someplace in my family roots; who can explain it? I might have forgotten about her, but I was occasionally conducting readings with a bunch of other actors, where we'd get together and read stage plays or screenplays that piqued our attention. I attended a reading of Shakespeare's Othello in a basement-level apartment, and Kathleen was playing Desdemona. When I peered up at the basement window during the reading, I noticed her boyfriend kneeling down and gazing in from the pavement. I got the impression he was hanging protectively over her, as if he was scared someone would swoop in and steal up his lovely girlfriend.

Kathleen and I began seeing each other casually. She was from Mill Valley, a beautiful town south of San Francisco. Besides being a great actor, she enjoyed kayaking and gymnastics. Perhaps having only one foot in her performing career gave her a unique color. She was offered large and prestigious roles, but she turned them down, and other stars took them. Kathleen preferred to go another route. What a gift she possesses. I was quite impressed with her in I Never Promised You a Rose Garden; if you saw it, you'll understand.

After a few months of dating, Kathleen and I went to supper at the Beverly Wilshire Hotel, where I stayed during Scarface to be closer to the set. She was talking to me at that supper, giving me a tale about her life, revealing herself more and telling me things that made me recognize her. She was talking about her life and her emotions in a way that helped me comprehend what I had sensed intuitively the first time I met her. Then it happened: the thunderbolt returned. It took me months to figure it out. We remained together for a few years after that, and it was a very loving relationship.

Kathleen was a source of comfort for me during Scarface. It was a pleasure to come home every night to someone I adored, who would tell me about her day, what she'd worked on, who she'd spoken with, and what annoyances she'd experienced. It would take my mind off my own work, the situation Scarface had put me in, the days spent being beaten by that insane character, the smoke, the blood, and the three-hundred-pound machine gun. We stayed together once I finished Scarface. We even went on a fantastic trip to Europe, where we traveled around in a van, almost like hitchhikers. It was a lovely period, and it felt so simple—unfettered, without fanfare. She was an excellent traveler who handled many tasks that I was and continue to be incapable of. We were also living together, which felt liberating in some ways. Our life together was manageable and easy.

My work on Scarface was completed in between productions of David Mamet's brilliant play American Buffalo. I spent a few years sporadically performing the play off Broadway at Circle in the Square, where we premiered it in 1981. We had been performing it in the round, but we were about to embark on a tour that would take us to San Francisco, Washington, D.C., Boston, and London, all of which had proscenium theatres. That meant we needed a proscenium theater to practice in, which is not always simple to find in New York. But in 1983, just before Scarface was out, we were given an incredible chance at the Booth Theatre, a stunning Broadway venue.

They also seemed to have a hard time with my co-star in the play, my dear, valued buddy Jimmy Hayden, who gave an outstanding performance. Jimmy was an excellent actress and a really attractive child. He was in his twenties and did not have a family of his own, yet I loved him as if we were related. He was also a drug addict. But he had a gift. He was both attractive and talented. He had it all. I've met folks like that my entire life; they just have that brilliance and wildness about them. They're vulnerable.

Jimmy's performance at American Buffalo was a genuine, breathing showcase—everyone who walked in noticed him. During the Broadway run, we lost Jimmy to drugs; this is how it always goes. It, of course, broke our hearts, and I still think about it now. When you're that close to someone and realize you've lost them, it hurts, and there's nothing you can do or say. Everyone thought Jimmy was going to go far.

When you are confident in something, criticism is sometimes easier to accept. These things can happen when you make movies. Some of them become contentious and are criticized by a segment of the public, and I can't for the life of me figure out why some of them get to live again. I had never seen a newspaper headline in huge, black, strong letters that screamed Pacino Fails Miserably as Scarface until I was approached by a lady who was eager to see me backstage at an American Buffalo performance. She wanted my autograph, so she grabbed it for me to sign. If that headline doesn't make your brain dance, I'm not sure what will. But this woman couldn't have cared less about the review. She could see into the future.

Rocky Bauer and I were both nominated for Golden Globes, but Scarface received little recognition at the Academy Awards. Brian De Palma did an amazing job with Scarface, charting the film and imbuing it with dynamism and reach. He pushed it to the maximum. I'll never understand why he wasn't recognized for this. When the Oscar nominations were released, I was in San Francisco doing American Buffalo at the Curran Theatre, where police officers on horseback helped handle the masses that waited after each play. On that day, when there were no nominations for my performance or anyone else's contributions to Scarface, a group of admirers approached me after the matinee and made their way past the cops to present me with a homemade Oscar they had manufactured to compensate for this apparent omission. It looked exactly like an actual Oscar, only bigger. It felt like the appropriate kind of honor, a trophy from the people, and I still have it now.

Scarface would eventually be adopted by the hip-hop generation, who identified with and validated Tony Montana's legend. Don't forget that Tony Montana was flying higher and higher until he burst, just like Icarus. Rappers and their followers embraced the film. They got it and went with the metaphor. They interpreted the film as a parable, a fable about how you perceive the world when you are taught that life is cheap and disposable. They served as the impetus and springboard for the film's eventual success, since once they bought it, the rest of the world did too.

People from many walks of life began discovering the film. Some hailed from low-income families, while others were elites, including college students, prison convicts, and professional sports. The film became counterculture. Tony Montana's legend extended globally. Tony Montana enables people to break free from themselves and their circumstances—break free from your rut, break free from life as you've been taught to live it. There is something wonderful about the voyage. That is why people who have lived in the world depicted in it can relate to it and survive it. They understood the drama's joke.

When Scarface celebrated its 35th anniversary in 2018, we staged a large reunion celebration at the Beacon Theatre in Manhattan. It was the final time I met Marty Bregman, who was 92 and in a wheelchair. He died a few weeks later. We had a sold-out audience of thousands of people, the majority of whom had seen it before but never on a large screen. I also invited a few pals who I knew weren't lovers of the film. I love, appreciate, and respect these folks, and they remain my friends.

When the film appeared on that large, magnificent screen, it seemed as if it had been sent into space. The vastness and magnificence of it became obvious. Even De Palma felt a stronger connection to the film. My buddies who had never liked Scarface before didn't remark it was the best picture they'd ever seen. They did notice, however, that it was rich. They accepted the essence of the thing, as I expected when they saw it with an audience. They were allowed to identify where the laughs, nuance, and drama were. Oh, that's what it implies. In other ways, the crowd served as subtitles for the film, supplying them with its inner language.

It remains the largest film I've ever made. The residuals continue to support me. I can live on it. I mean, I could if I lived a normal life. But, simply put, it helps. I believe that if Scarface were released tomorrow, it would elicit the same emotion and spark the same discussion. It's just too cumbersome. This is all there is.

Chapter 9: It's Over

I was out. My movie career is over. What I had built up, role by role, was lost in a matter of years. Each subsequent failure seemed like a bigger weight pressing down on my chest. I started questioning the core substance of what I was doing and why I was doing it. I felt stuck, creatively drained, and disconnected from the reasons I became an actor in the first place.

So I quit. No notice was given and no comment made. I just stopped accepting film parts. I didn't care. I answered, "This is fine." I still have a lot to be grateful for. I've got New York. I have my friends. I can read plays all day and still have a choice about what to do. But when it came to flicks, I was done. I made a few blunders when I quit. One was that I assumed I could return whenever I wanted. However, people are far more ready to move on without you than you know. When you're counted out, you're out, and that's especially true if you appear to be uninterested in returning.

I was working on the film Revolution in England just before I retired. Every day in Norfolk, I awoke on a farm. I was a hundred miles from London and distant from anywhere that felt familiar. The property was not luxurious; it was simply a worn-out cottage in the British countryside. Every step I took was greeted with creaking floors. A king's ransom for used furniture. But it can also be charming. I enjoyed waking up to the sunlight and the sounds of farm animals. Horses and cows. Fucking geese. But horses and cows.

I'm not sure what went wrong with the Revolution. Sometimes it's simply the usual suspects. I must admit that I admired the director, Hugh Hudson, a British filmmaker who had recently won an Oscar for Chariots of Fire. When he told me about the project, he used a very compelling tone. The film Revolution would follow the story of a gruff father who has been knocked around by life and comes to New York with his young kid on the day that America declares independence from Great Britain. Hudson promised a vivid and unsentimental recreation of colonial life, and Charlie pushed me to execute it after we spoke about the script for a long period.

Aside from driving me out of the film profession, Revolution derailed a brilliant director's career. Hugh Hudson was a skilled artist, but his dogmatic approach alienated others, and when the picture tanked, the industry blamed him. He had a difficult time in his career subsequently. Its failure lingered with both of us for a long time, and it knocked Goldcrest Films off the rankings.

Hugh Hudson and I continued to collaborate for twenty years after Revolution was released, seeking new methods to work on the picture, adding elements we felt were lacking, and trimming it down where we could. We collected our own funds, and I commissioned friends to write some of the voice-over narration. After Hugh died, a few hundred people attended a special screening of the film's new edit, Revolution: Revisited, at the Aero Theatre in Santa Monica. When you watched it on a screen that big and in a theater with those acoustics, you saw a brilliant director do something spectacular. These new adjustments improved Revolution: Revisited and gave it a resonance that audiences did not have forty years before, thanks to the added narrative and editing. The updated version looked great on the Aero's enormous, gorgeous screen.

When I stopped working commercially, I returned to plays and ideas that had piqued my interest long before my time in Hollywood. As a young man, Heathcote Williams' one-act drama, The Local Stigmatic attracted me. Now, in my middle age, it transported me back to those bohemian days, to the exact ethos of the world that had inspired me as a teenager on my first visit to the Village. I hadn't realized how much it had inspired me during my time at the Living Theatre and other performing places, and I wanted to explore and process it.

Williams was 21 when he wrote it. After a lot of small talk and humorous lines, they begin walking the actor home, and the energy shifts and becomes threatening. One of the gamblers delivers a monologue in which he alleges the actor saw him on the street but pretended not to recognize him. The men hurl him to the ground and begin kicking him. They do not kill him, but they do leave a cut on his face. The mark is symbolic—it expresses their presence and existence. The Local Stigmatic tells a story about identification and envy. It's about those among us who have a need to be noticed and how it might make others envious. Heathcote was discussing how that affects specific types of people who feel on the margins. He was only a child when he wrote it, but he understood it and expressed it well in the play. These notions can be difficult for audiences to accept.

Heathcote, whom I befriended, was a vivacious, furious intellectual, an Oxford graduate, a gorgeous poet and painter, and a staunch political anarchist. He was my British Cliffy. He enjoyed performing magic acts. He lived in a treehouse and dated model Jean Shrimpton. I traversed the streets of London with him as he carried two shopping bags, God alone knows what was inside. As we sat down for tea at some eccentric restaurant, we came into Rudolf Nureyev, possibly the finest ballet dancer of all time, who told us how much he adored Scarface. That was a lift I needed. That got me through my entire trip in England.

Years later, Heathcote assisted me on the film The Devil's Advocate. They ate it up. Then Heathcote requested screen credit—just a mention, not as one of the primary writers, of course—but this was impossible for them to provide. So I paid Heathcote out of my own wallet, which was not impossible and completely worthwhile. We shot The Local Stigmatic in Atlanta for a few weeks, with David Wheeler directing and a principal cast that included myself, Paul Guilfoyle, Joe Maher, and Michael Higgins. When the film was ready, we presented it to people we admired. We attended a wonderful dinner gathering of artists and literati in London. People like Tom Stoppard and David Hare sat at a large table. Harold Pinter had watched the picture twice by this stage; he sat at the head of the table, and when he wished to address everyone, he rang a small bell, and the group became silent. He'd been labeled as Pinter's protégé, but being in the same room as his literary idol must have been too much for him.

And then one day, visiting another editing bay, I overheard it. I heard the same chuckle I heard on the set of The Godfather, when we had to convince ourselves that we weren't about to give up our careers. I saw the smile that convinced me during all those endless screen checks that I was safe and that someone was there to protect me, and the eyes that had seen and recognized me. Diane Keaton was working on her own picture. I have always liked women, but I've been shy around them since I was very little. I do not woo them. I do not seek them. Women either reply to you or not, and if they do not initiate contact with me, I am hesitant to attempt again. However, Diane's situation was different. We've always had a connection. She grasped my perspective, and it was reassuring to have someone who got me. So I went after her. We dated for a few months before deciding to meet. We found an appropriate tempo and temperature.

Diane was working extremely steadily at the time, making commercially successful films. When she appeared in Baby Boom, it was a huge success for her. Having a partner who was more accomplished than me didn't bother or intimidate me. I wasn't especially driven to get back into the game or adjust my attitude to my own projects. I merely wished Diane happiness with her profession, which she had. She'd go off to make a film for a few weeks, while I'd sit at home and read a play. I knew she was an artist, and I liked the various ways she used her skills as an actor, singer, writer, and photographer.

I brought Diane to my father's recent wedding in Los Angeles. He was a highly smart and resourceful man who had opened his own bar, restaurant, and nightclub in West Covina, which he named—what else?—Pacino's. The wedding was a real melting pot. I mean, talk about diversity—you've never seen so many people and children of all kinds, including all of my half brothers and half sisters from my father's prior marriages. The man preferred to settle down. He was married five times. No, not once. I suppose we balanced each other out that way.

Diane owned a house in California, which I adored. I went in and out as my tired, weepy self, and everything was OK. Perhaps that is what I was supposed to be, a look back at my life before I was known, when I spent it reading, thinking, strolling, and conversing. In New York, I could wander through Central Park on a regular basis, and I saw that as time passed, people glanced away from me. That took some getting used to, but there was something about it that brought me comfort.

That man was not the only one to bring this to my attention. While Marthe Keller was visiting me in New York, she mentioned it on another walk in Central Park. It was always Central Park; such a wonderful site. I was too delighted. I suppose it has been a long time since I made a film that most people could watch. I appreciated what these people were saying. I was tickled by the thought that my absence was not only noticed by certain individuals, but also had an impact on their life, because I was feeling fine. I felt free to interact, dabble, travel, and absorb what was happening to me after what felt like twenty years on hold. When I reflect on this period now, I am moved and miss it. It was a departure from something I wasn't particularly happy with. Being with Diane contributed significantly to my sense of serenity and contentment. I'd found the kind of comfort that allows you to feel and think about the world. I appreciated the freedom to pursue this exploratory trip without having to meet anyone's expectations other than my own, if I so desired. But I wouldn't have a choice for much longer.

I had somehow managed to run out of money. I looked up, and I didn't have any money. I may argue I was taken advantage of. I could blame the accountants. I might blame Marty Bregman, who had put me in some type of tax shelter that went wrong. I could blame myself, but that would require me to accept responsibility for my own acts. Anyway, I checked the cupboard and it was empty. I only had around $90,000 in the bank. Also, I led a lifestyle. I didn't want to give up my home in the country. I was spending without earning; I was putting out but not bringing in. I believe there is a word for that.

My entertainment lawyer, Arthur Klein, was a nice person. He sat me and Diane in his office, which was customarily furnished with family portraits and baseball memorabilia. Arthur began to explain that I had become insolvent due to poor asset management. I am aware that he was not involved. But words just washed over me.

Diane, however, was enraged.

She was referring to my financial situation—where I came from, my upbringing, my early life, and everything up to that point. And she was correct. I didn't grasp how money or careers worked. It was a language I didn't know. It didn't matter if I had to put everything back together. I had support. I had friends. I had Charlie. I knew I had the ability to return to work because I had received offers during my four-year absence from the film industry. What had stuck with me and drove me was a beeline. I could trace it all the way back to the night I stood on stage at the Actors Gallery to appear in Strindberg's Creditors. That moment when I told myself I could accomplish anything now. And I don't need to be wealthy, successful, or famous. I know I have it. It's a desire to do this. It will serve me anyhow. When you are hungry, you will find a way. I'll wait until I discover my tribe. Diane was even more encouraging.

With Diane's encouragement, I began to reconnect with the film industry. I acquired an agent who couldn't do much for me, but he tried. He brought me to Los Angeles to meet one of the studio's executives. We drove past one of those spectacular security gates, onto the lot, and were shown into his offices. You could see it took a lot of effort for this guy to meet with me; he was running late and had us waiting in an outlying chamber—not even his inner room—for forty-five minutes before he arrived. I had been nominated for five Oscars by this point, yet my agent acted as if I was looking for a handout.

I then began pitching a story about Edmund Kean, the great British actor from the early 1800s, his insane life, and all that had occurred to him. I felt that would make an intriguing, humorous, and heartbreaking film. I said that there were biographies of Kean and plays based on his exploits, and I'd be pleased to provide them to the executive so he could better grasp Edmund Kean's extraordinary talent and life. The executive stayed silent and looked at me as if I were a recovering leper who was ready to become contagious in front of his eyes. You know how some people can express themselves without saying anything? But, to be honest, I knew this wasn't going to end well the moment I walked into his office. That was the first and last time I attended such a meeting. I never found the right words to express myself in that environment of business people and others who work in that field. That's all foreign to me.

We spent the summer shooting Sea of Love in Toronto. Though I had previously played romantic leads in other films, this film is best known for a long, languid sex scene in which Ellen Barkin pushes me against a wall and gives me a pat-down before our two characters begin their affair. Becker staged the situation well.

I don't normally play graphic love scenes, and I don't think many other actors do either. It can get borderline pornographic. I realize it's pointless for me to lament that we're no longer in the era of films like

A Place in the Sun, where Elizabeth Taylor and Montgomery Clift could have an entire audience swooning in their seats without ever seeing their nude bodies.

Sea of Love is an excellent Hollywood picture, a commercial film, and a showcase for Harold Becker's talents. It's all held together by a very thin wire of belief. There are a few minor flaws in the tale, but I'm not going to point them out. It was a significant boost for actors like Richard Jenkins and John Goodman, who were not well-known at the time. Ellen Barkin delivered a sensational and artistic performance that tore the screen apart. I felt lucky to be part of it. The picture earned $100 million out of nowhere. For the first time in a long time, I was part of a successful film. I didn't make much money since I didn't have an appropriate back end, which meant I didn't have any at all. They knew I'd been out of commission for four years, so they didn't have to offer such a good deal. They know when you're down. But I moved from having no money to having some again. I had plenty of opportunities to act in films again, and produce and direct a couple more. As I discovered in Hollywood, not wanting something sometimes is the best way to obtain it.

Chapter 10: Just When I Thought I Was Out

In 1990, I was still riding the wave of Sea of Love. They were making a huge fuss over me at the photo shoot because The Godfather: Part III was going to come out. More than fifteen years after the second and seemingly final installment in the cinematic story that drew me out of the shadows and tossed me into the arena with the lions, a third chapter was on its way. Francis Ford Coppola was back. I was back. Michael Corleone would return. Then the editors at People magazine saw The Godfather: Part III, and wouldn't you know it, I was removed from the magazine's cover. I did not get any story at all. It was canceled and died on arrival. The photo shoot was sabotaged. I had been given the red carpet treatment, and it was gone in the blink of an eye. All that time I spent in front of the camera, writhing like an insect like the guy in the Kafka story, was for naught.

Nonetheless, after being practically written off in Hollywood, I was ready to make a comeback. You know how it goes: everyone enjoys seeing you fall from your perch, but nothing beats a comeback story. Perhaps it was my ego, but I didn't see it as a comeback, although it was portrayed as such. I simply returned to work. The Godfather: Part III almost derailed the resurgence that began with Sea of Love. The audience had issues with it, but throughout the course of my four subsequent films, I found myself a different guy. I've matured. At the end of that run, I was ready to stop hiding from my background, let my guard down a little, and embrace the plaudits and acclaim I had been avoiding during my early achievements.

Dick Tracy was fantastic, and working with Warren was pure delight because he just lets you run wild. When he's in charge, he'll give you as many takes as you want, and his sense of direction is impeccable. He will always make you appear better, therefore you can't go wrong. Dick Tracy was a lovely film, energized by Dick Sylbert's production design and Vittorio Storaro's photography. I had a fresh desire to use my imagination and create a character with a true identity. I had my own concept about this individual. They nicknamed him Big Boy because he had elephantiasis. Parts of him were swollen to an abnormal degree. Oversized hands. A jutting chin. A bulbous nose. John Caglione Jr., the makeup artist, and I experimented with various designs that we planned to present to Warren. I became extremely grotesque at one point, and Warren convinced me to tone it down a little.

This was still the beginning of the era of comic-book and comic-strip characters being made into films, and this one eluded the youthful audience. It was enjoyable and profitable, but it did not quite live up to its stated box office promise. It possessed wit and sophistication. I didn't even take billing for the character; I was just having fun with it. And it earned me my first Oscar nomination in almost a decade. However, as I may have indicated, it was not the only film I produced that year.

The issues began shortly after. There was an issue with Robert Duvall, and he refused to do the picture. These things occur. In Part II, Richard Castellano, who played Clemenza, did not return. I virtually begged Richard to do it since he was so good at playing Clemenza, but he refused. Why exactly was never explained. I never understood why Duvall didn't want to do it again. Either way, his absence from Part III was a significant loss. We didn't know what to do without him because his character was vital to the film. Francis and Mario had to rewrite the tale, but they were superb writers who reworked the entire script. Even the finale that I adored had to go— instead, Michael would die in old age, alone, after his daughter, Mary, is killed in an effort to assassinate him.

Winona Ryder was meant to play Mary, but when she arrived in Rome, she was fatigued and distraught. Sofia Coppola ended up playing the role. She was just nineteen years old and had no experience as an actress, but we later discovered she is a really great director. However, the rest of the cast was attempting to manage this as we were learning a completely new screenplay for the picture. You had Andy Garcia, the wonderful actor, playing Vincent, Sonny's bastard son. He was a rugged, handsome guy who could seduce a woman with the snap of his fingers. Now he's attempting to pursue the boss's daughter. And to top it off, she is his first cousin.

Eli Wallach and I would have terrific card games outside at night on the steps of the beautiful old Sicilian buildings where we were filming. George Hamilton, who was written into the picture as a character to replace Tom Hagen and who also happens to be one of the greatest people I've ever met, took me to London during a break in production. I spent four days in a hotel recovering from the virus, except for a few nights out with George. We hit the roulette tables in some opulent casinos and danced the night away. I felt like a college kid who had been kicked out of a dormitory.

When we returned to Rome, I was in the rear lot of Cinecittà studios, enjoying a break because they hadn't finished my scenes yet. I was alone, and I felt a depression creep up on me. Melancholia was what I preferred to call it. I felt like I was roaming around in the role of Michael and had lost my appetite, which I was used to having when performing in a film. That could have been cause for my grief. I was looking for a solution to rekindle my appetite and attitude.

The notion would not leave me. So I will continue to ponder it. And so I stated to myself, "The only way to understand what this is is to try it." Create a film of Richard III and constantly interrupt it with vignettes of people discussing it—actors, famous writers, and people on the street—while we prepped and performed the play. It was a huge collage with me in the center. I don't consider myself a director or writer. But there was a need for me to communicate all this, and just thinking about it was helping me feel better. Color was returning to my cheeks. If I recall properly, I noticed my own shoelaces tie themselves. I pondered it throughout the 1990s. Finally, I determined that the only way I'd grasp it was to go out and begin filming it. But this would have to wait.

When David Mamet's Glengarry Glen Ross premiered on Broadway in the mid-1980s, I was offered the role of Ricky Roma, the show's leading real estate dealer. Joe Mantegna performed so well on stage that he earned a Tony Award. So I was fortunate that they contacted me years later for the film adaptation, which was directed by Jamie Foley, who was also very engaged in the casting. When you're around Jack Lemmon, Alec Baldwin, Alan Arkin, Ed Harris, Kevin Spacey, and Jonathan Pryce, you know you're in good hands. And they gave us three weeks of practice before production began, which seemed like a gift, and by the time we started shooting the film in Queens, we were really flying.

Marty Brest told me about Scent of a Woman. Marty is a kind guy and an excellent director who had already made Beverly Hills Cop and Midnight Run by that point. I read Bo Goldman's latest draft for the American adaptation. I actually read it aloud at one point. The script was good. I completed my homework. I completed my preparation. Then I started to work. And I had to go through a lot to play Lieutenant Colonel Frank Slade, the main character in Scent of a Woman. He was a spouter. He was a genuine pisspot. An alcoholic and an absolute despot. He was simply nuts. He intended to commit suicide. The entire objective of his trip to New York, for which he hires the brilliant Chris O'Donnell to be his assistant, is to say goodbye to individuals. However, it is neither sentimental nor self-pitying. Slade's intentions are cold and plain, as is the weight of his depression, and I believe you have to die spiritually, inside yourself, before you kill yourself. Marty Brest was the one who truly captured that—he was so amazing at keeping me in control and modulating my performance, and he is a great guy. I did go overboard at times throughout that section. Sometimes I was too large for it. I would become too out of control. I can do it better now.

My first child, Julie Marie Pacino, was born in October 1989. Though I had to swiftly acclimate to the responsibilities of fatherhood, I genuinely enjoyed being a father. Julie attended the Little Red Schoolhouse in the West Village when she was very small, and after school, I would take her to an Italian restaurant around the corner. We'd sit outside and eat, and she'd tell me about her day. When people came by and started talking to me, she would simply slip under the table. I had two Oscar nominations that same year, for Glengarry Glen Ross (my seventh) and Scent of a Woman (my eighth). I felt flattered and grateful. But then the chatter around me shifted. I'd never won one, so people started talking about me as if it were my turn. How many times could I be rejected?

As I reflected on it, I determined that, sure, I will take this seriously. It's time for me to accept some responsibility and embrace the situation with grace. I recruited a fantastic PR named Pat Kingsley. I've never had one before. I wasn't even sure what they were. I didn't give many TV interviews, especially after an episode in the 1980s when I was convinced to do a morning discussion show for Scarface. But the guy approached me with a disdainful expression, white as a ghost, and asked how I could have made a film like Scarface. You try to respond to the inquiry. I began meeting her in public places throughout New York. We met together in a café. I met her at the rear of a soda pop luncheonette. She was lovely, and I liked her a lot, but she was obviously trying to convince me to be on her show. Eventually, I agreed to do it.

Initially, I was shocked by the interview findings. I was present but not there. I was like someone hiding behind the curtains while conducting an interview. I wondered how you could be on a talk program and not say anything. But when I watched it again recently, I discovered it wasn't all that horrible. Okay, I looked a little shy. And she was really classy, so we got up and danced the tango. And there were many people watching. I must admit I looked handsome. They realized I was human, and I said things that were human. So it is very excellent.

I felt out of place when I attended the Oscars for Serpico. When I returned twenty years later, I was in exactly the same condition. I was still out of place. I hadn't created that part of yourself that comes to life and allows you to accept your current situation. Someone recently informed me that Jack Kerouac was quite embarrassed about his fame. That's a complicated topic, but I've been thinking about how it might apply to me. I like hearing the tale about Kerouac because if someone like him could feel that way, it lends legitimacy to my position.

I sat there, glassy-eyed and motionless, as they announced my name and the other contenders for Best Actor. But, as they revealed my name as the winner, I had a sense they'd finally do it. I tossed back my head and sighed. That made many chuckle, but it was also true. It was a genuinely moving experience to watch the entire audience come up and applaud me, and my thanks was genuine.

But on the plane, a feeling overcame me. It was similar to what I experienced when I first entered the Actors Studio as a child. I was standing on a subway platform when I boarded the approaching train and looked around to see the doors close. I noticed my reflection in the metro car window and assumed I was an actor. I'm a member of Actors Studio. Sitting alone on the plane, I had a sense of resolution. It was a deep gift, and it's difficult to put into words because you're so emotional. I think this is what it means to feel good about yourself—you're not sure why, but you do. It felt like being one of those hang gliders I've seen diving off the cliffs in Montauk—after being up in the air for so long, there's a relief in eventually touching down, and mercifully it doesn't stay too long. When you win an Oscar, everyone knows you've accomplished something remarkable and treats you accordingly for approximately a week. I guess that's why we have holidays like Mother's Day and Father's Day. We need to be slapped on the back for doing something useful despite everything we've been through.

Chapter 11: Forty Dollars a Day (and All the Donuts You Can Eat)

The first film in this series was Carlito's Way, a Marty Bregman special. I was back on familiar territory, filming in New York and reuniting with Marty, my trusted producer, and Brian De Palma, a brilliant filmmaker; it was also my first time working with Sean Penn and Penelope Ann Miller, who were all fantastic. It was a mini Scarface reunion for myself, Marty, and Brian, but we weren't attempting to recreate what we did in that film, and Carlito Brigante couldn't have been more different from Scarface as a character. He does not get high. He does not lose his cool. He keeps his cool. He is eventually brought down by a major fault in his personality, when he gives mercy to a rival he certainly shouldn't have.

I collaborated with Marty Bregman on five films, including Serpico, Dog Day Afternoon, Scarface, Sea of Love, and Carlito's Way. All were successes, but Carlito was the final film we made together. We didn't break up or have a falling out this time; we simply parted ways. He had goals he wanted to achieve, and I had mine. By this point, I was convinced that I would only make a gangster picture if the character was something I had never done before. That was true for Donnie Brasco, which I created years later. Lefty Ruggiero, my guy, was a Mafia made man, which is no minor feat. But Lefty was at the bottom of his organization's hierarchy, with no hope of moving up. Carlito Brigante was a gangster, a street person, but he was also a romantic and an outsider. Lefty had an almost sorrowful quality to him that I believed I had never played before.

The year before, I had made Heat, my first picture with Michael Mann. This time I played a cop, a Los Angeles police lieutenant named Vincent Hanna. Hanna faced challenges as a human being and in his life. He was temperamental, edgy, and prone to going insane. He was also using cocaine, and I based my entire character on it. We shot a sequence in which I went into a club, and you could see my character take a smack of drugs before entering. For whatever reason, Michael left the moment from the film. It did explain a lot of my character's behavior, and without that explanation, I can understand how certain portions of my performance appeared exaggerated. If the audience had witnessed a few moments where Hanna took a hit, I believe they would have been better prepared to see what I did. Even without it, Hanna's life was intense—how he worked in his career, how he dealt with things—giving him the ability to use that type of energy. It was almost like a detective technique, and it worked well for him.

I recall meeting Bob many years ago, when Jill Clayburgh and I were living in the Village. We were walking down Fourteenth Street when we came across a few people she knew. One was a young man with an unusually intense personality. He had a distance about him—he didn't look you directly in the eyes—but he exuded charisma. And that was Bob. Jill introduced me to him and said he was an excellent actor. I knew he had that gift; I could see it in passing. He seemed to recognize some of the theatrical stuff I'd been doing. We shook hands, wished each other well, and went on our way.

Then there are all the ways we've been compared to each other, paired together, and portrayed as competitors, just because we're performers who appeared on the scene around the same time and have last names that end in a vowel. We have certain things in common, but we are as different as any two individuals can be. And there was competition among us. There had to be. Especially when the offers were comparable; roles that might have been played by any of us. The spot of competition can only be found there.

Over the years, Bob and I would try to find ways to collaborate on a film, but we never seemed to find the perfect project. When Bob was cast in Bernardo Bertolucci's 1900, he approached me about working with him. Bob was being encouraging. When Michael Mann approached Bob and me with the screenplay for Heat, he told us that we could play either Hanna, the cop, or McCauley, the robber. It turned out that Bob wanted the thief and I wanted the cop. Then we had a screenplay reading with Bob, Val Kilmer, Jon Voight, and many more outstanding performers gathered around the table. Bob was playing a very powerful character, but I could tell he was delivering a more restrained and low-key performance, focused and lonely. It was beautiful. I knew I'd go in the opposite direction.

Michael Mann chose me and Bob because he didn't want two guys who were alike; he wanted a contrast. He was building up the tension for a scene halfway through the film in which we sit down together in a restaurant and talk for the first time. When it came time to shoot the restaurant scene, Bob refused to rehearse it. And I thought, He was correct. We arrived and were just getting started. We didn't think about it or discuss it; it was there. It was quite wise of Bob to do it that way.

Looking for Richard has begun to take shape since I first imagined it in Godfather III. I was able to fulfill my dreams. I did it with my own money, so I didn't have to answer to anyone or follow the many restrictions that apply when people invest in your film and want their money back. An art film is a bet, and you cannot expect to recoup your investment or be disappointed if this does not occur. They are not intended to be commercial; rather, they serve a different type of audience. To be really honest, part of me wanted to produce this film to exorcise my sentiments about how I was treated on Broadway when I performed Richard III, and critics said I set Shakespeare back fifty years in this nation. And part of me did it out of reverence for artists such as Orson Welles, the true master of the cinema medium. He did everything in his career. His entire life was spent piecemealing pictures, constantly raising funds to make them, and never receiving the attention he deserved for them. I'd never dare to compare myself to Welles, but he influenced me, and I'd like to believe I had a genuine Welles experience when I made Looking for Richard.

Everything about it energized me. There's a certain enthusiasm that comes with doing something where you don't have to sit around waiting to be called to go do your taxes. When you watch Looking for Richard, you'll see me figuring out how to direct a scene while still acting in it. The cameras are rolling, the scene is in progress, and I'm acting, directing, and ducking out of frame to encourage the cameraman to move in on a shot, all while managing the movement of other actors with hand signals and gestures like a third-base coach. There's a cyclone of acting and directing going on, and I'm enjoying being calm in the midst of it all.

During the filming of Looking for Richard, I took my cast and crew to the Cloisters and the Cathedral of St. John the Divine, where I met Philippe Petit, the astonishing tightrope artist with arms like cables and incredible strength. He had walked on a high wire from a building across the street to the cathedral's roof, 150 feet above the ground, without a net. Remember that. I had planned to bring my actors in Looking for Richard up to the church's top, but then I noticed all the pigeon poo, which I had read, was exceedingly dangerous. Someone on set also mentioned it.

We eventually discovered a filming location for Richard's brother Clarence's murder that was free of pigeon poo. It wasn't the magnificent piece of architecture that St. John the Divine is—it didn't make me feel like I was in the realm of Michelangelo, a setting where you believe you can accomplish anything. I assumed that was where Shakespeare belonged. But we discovered another setting uptown on the East Side that was actually better. We could now kill Clarence. The people in charge of the church were gracious enough to let me film there for free. Doing the medieval scenes in the city was a fantastic experience. New York had already given me so much, and it was now giving me even more. I will never forget that.

We needed to conduct one of those market research screenings for the film. It wasn't just my buddies who were looking at it; these were complete strangers who had been chosen as potential fans of the wild things I did. I wasn't sure what they expected to see. Suppose they booed or simply departed in response to this thing in which I've poured so much of my heart and soul. All I could think was, "My film is really bad." As I sat there, I hoped that, somehow, as the film moved from the editing room to the theater where we were showing it, some modifications would be made to make it better. The audience would rise from their seats and cheer. Then I got a better idea: I will prevent people from coming at all.

Looking for Richard received some attention, but its failure to thrive pained me personally. It wasn't simply a letdown. It was a life-changing event. You can be doing well in life, but then you encounter rejection, which utterly overshadows all of your previous achievements. I didn't really address that disappointment at the time since it's difficult to deal with when it happens.

Many years later, after relocating from New York to Los Angeles to be closer to my ex and children, I found myself at a party next door to the property I was renting. The hostess who lived there was a bit of a hotshot in her own right, but as I got to know her, I discovered that she was a pretty decent human being in general. One night, she hosted a large number of celebrities and well-known producers from Hollywood's upper echelon. I met a couple of them and realized that nobody knew about Looking for Richard. Here's a film I wrote, directed, and starred in, with a cast of excellent British and American performers who wowed the audience with their talents. The Directors Guild of America awarded me Best Director for Looking for Richard, and The New York Times rated it one of the year's top ten films. But no one at that party knew. They had never seen it or heard of it.

After Looking for Richard, I didn't perform Shakespeare again for nearly a decade, until I played Shylock in a 2004 film adaptation of The Merchant of Venice. I believed its director, Michael Radford, had made some excellent pictures. And its producer, Barry Navidi, approached me about it after working on another film with Marlon Brando and Johnny Depp. I could see Barry had a solid brain and a natural knowledge of the performer and the art form of filmmaking. He knew Brando well, and he stated Marlon had recommended that I play Shylock. I have no idea how Marlon saw that in me.

I knew Dustin Hoffman had played Shylock on Broadway and in London, but what struck me most about The Merchant of Venice was the perception that it was antisemitic. That notoriety dates back to its inception over four hundred years ago and has been passed down since then. However, our audience has shifted. In certain ways, the drama is relevant to the present era. When we observe Shylock being prejudiced, we understand why. Many of us can relate to his situation. I'm not Jewish, but I saw Shylock as a man relegated to a ghetto and tormented by bigots. Not only do they humiliate and spit on him, but they also abduct his precious daughter, which was all he had in the world. Nonetheless, he carries himself with dignity. He feels vindicated by what happened to him. He is not Iago, Richard III, or any other Shakespearean villain. He has a heroic quality to him. He is a survivor. I believed that our world today has room for that, and that a film about it would be important.

It took me months to get to that performance—months of rehearsing, filming it, and doing it in Central Park. I believe I profited from the time I spent with it, which gave me a sense of independence and contributed to my Tony nomination, which was quite fulfilling. When I work on something for a long time, I can discover the character within me. I still want to play Shylock again, maybe in England. Shylock is one of the great actors' parts, and it helped Edmund Kean establish his career. When he performed Shylock, people were so taken aback that they ran out of the theater during the play and into the street, telling passers-by to come in and take a look.

Chapter 12: You Can Always Buy New Friends

2001 started on a good note. Beverly D'Angelo and I had fraternal twins—a boy and a girl. Beverly and I had disagreements over where to live. Her life was almost entirely spent in Los Angeles. New York was my home, and I had always intended to stay there. My physician cautioned me not to move to Los Angeles. I went anyway. There I was in my early sixties, starting a new life in a new city. I had no idea how to traverse Los Angeles. I didn't grasp the social scene. I knew I could return to New York as much as possible.

In Los Angeles, I moved multiple times with my two young children while figuring out where to reside. We outgrew one apartment after the next. Beverly and I were navigating the complexities of raising our children apart. There were visitations scheduled, and the children would remain with one parent or the other for a while before we settled on 50/50 custody. Even yet, my work required me to be away from them on occasion. Given all my children had to go through, I am grateful that they came out so well. They didn't always get the attention they wanted or deserved from me, and while I tried to interact with them as much as possible, once a family has been destroyed, it's always more difficult. As much as I understand it now, I wish I had known it then.

Los Angeles was considerably different from New York, and a New Yorker outside of New York is considered an alien. There was a lot more interaction in Los Angeles. There is a sense of community, but there are specific laws that must be followed depending on whatever area you are in. Beverly Hills is large, yet parts of its areas resemble a country club—a massive one with parties and banquets, and you fumble your way around in the dark. At first, I was frightened of going out alone because I would always get lost and be unable to find my way home. But many areas of Los Angeles were lovely and hospitable, and I was fortunate to meet individuals I liked. My longtime friend Harold Becker and his wife lived in Los Angeles, and they were always quite cordial to me. Harold toured me about the city.

Los Angeles is relatively provincial. It is provincial, like other places, with its core identity derived from its employment source. In Los Angeles, the primary source of employment is film production. It's an industrial town, and the industry is show business. You're never far from the people you work with, and some will judge you based not only on the work you do, but also on the reputation you've built up over time. A few weeks later, I attended another party, a post-Oscars celebration in Century City, which was held in an apartment with a panoramic view of the Hollywood skyline. It was a pretty classy place, and everyone and everybody was present. I was thoroughly enjoying myself, and there were plenty of fascinating people to talk to. I actually met Oprah Winfrey that night. I was leaving the party with a buddy when I observed a woman I knew—a talented actress—holding a drink and crying. When you're talking to someone and weighing your words, spontaneity may leave the building. As I stared at the grieving woman, I felt for her and thought, "That is a strange feeling."

So I met this guy one night at a restaurant while sowing my oats. I wasn't drinking anymore, but I still had some crazy going on inside me, doing the old coin flip. I was on a high, engaged in repartee and surprising myself that I could still do that at the age of sixty. I just met him off the cuff and had no idea who he was. But I had a great time with this big-name fella, and I had a strong need to show off that night. I wasn't trying, and sometimes that's the finest way to be. Days later, I received a call from my agent. He told me that so-and-so now wants to meet me in his office high above Hollywood—he was with you the other night and thought you were hilarious.

At the same time, I discovered ways to entertain myself in Los Angeles. I had pals, and everything was fine. I stated, "I don't want to be here just hanging out." You can only play so much paddle tennis. My life was becoming increasingly expensive—my workforce was growing, and I was managing two homes, apartments, and an office, and supporting my children's households. I was spending three or four hundred thousand dollars per month, which was a lot of money. I wanted to stay active, so I made a few films here and there. I believe I've gotten off track. I suppose I need one of those 500-pound gorillas to pull me back in. That's what Charlie used to say to me while we were wandering the streets of New York, along the sidewalks and bridges, bouncing like a couple of errant vagabonds practicing for a marathon, quoting Dylan Thomas, Allen Ginsberg, or my favorite, "Jingle Bells."

After moving to Los Angeles, I still needed to satisfy my own artistic desires, and I could feel them again. So I began making another of my own films, similar to Looking for Richard. This time, I chose Oscar Wilde's Salomé, a piece that had always piqued my interest and that I had previously performed at Circle in the Square. I adored Wilde and this play, so I embarked on a nearly ten-year journey to create the film Wilde Salomé, which explored the life of Oscar Wilde as I was performing the play Salomé onstage at night and filming a version of the play in a studio during the day. Wilde Salomé says a lot about what was going on in my life at the time, while I was raising my children and adjusting to this new location. Barry Navidi, who produced the film The Merchant of Venice, was also living in Los Angeles. Barry is a lovely person to deal with. He is honest and knowledgeable about cinema. He was also foolish enough to agree with me and my admiration for Oscar Wilde. It took me years to film it in Los Angeles while also performing in other projects. I was juggling a lot while raising my children, who appear in the film as well.

Beyond what I was spending on Wilde Salomé, I was throwing money about because I had it. At least, I believed I did. And my accountant kept encouraging me. I was doing what many individuals do who have no idea about money and are ignorant. My seven-year-old daughter once had a schoolmate whose father worked as an actor and needed money. "Okay, what do you need?" I asked. I gave him $65 thousand. I didn't anticipate anything back. I'd do that a lot. I wasn't doing it to prove that I was charitable; I simply thought I had a lot to share. To me, it was like winning Monopoly. This wasn't real. None of it seemed real to me. But it's real. I was to find out.

I was getting signals that my accountant at the time, a person with a lot of celebrity customers, could not be trusted. In 2011, I was sitting in the living room of my Beverly Hills rental house, doing something I rarely did: reviewing my finances. I pay a ridiculous amount of money to rent a big luxury mansion in Beverly Hills because I always think it's only temporary and that I'll move somewhere else or do something different. Of course I haven't, yet I've been renting the same place for the past twenty years. You don't have to be an accountant to see it's a bad waste of money, but the fact that he didn't point it out should have been a warning.

By this point, my suspicions had grown, and my unscrupulous accountant had not come to visit me. He almost never did; he always dispatched one of his subordinates. I'm uneasy when I'm around stuff I don't feel related to or know much about. I was sitting at a table, reviewing my notes, and the minion representing my accountant was sitting behind me.

The money I was spending and where it was going was a bizarre collage of loss. The door was wide open, and I had no idea who was living off of me. Even after being duped like that, I still owe gift taxes on all the money I gave people. Even though I only had two cars, I was apparently paying for sixteen, and twenty-three cell phones that I had no idea existed. The landscaper was paid $400,000 a year to landscape a house I didn't even reside in. I don't overstate these facts. It simply went on and on. I wasn't even signing my own checks; the accountant did it, and I just let them go. I wasn't looking, and he didn't tell me how much I had or where it was going. I also wasn't keeping track of who got what. It was all about keeping this foolish actor pleased; just keep him working, and we'll reap the benefits. It turned out that this individual was also uninsured, so I couldn't sue him for damages.

I played it like I had a lot more money than I did. My fiancée, Lucila, was quite supportive at the time, as did many of my friends and others close to me. I went into survival mode, which is something I am capable of doing. I've lived a life that has given me the means to survive. By now, I was in my seventies. I wasn't a young buck, and I wasn't going to make as much money from performing in films as I had in the past. The hefty paychecks that I was used to weren't rolling in anymore. The pendulum has swung, and I found it harder to find bits for myself. I suppose it's what all performers go through: as they get older, their roles get fewer. I'd have to perform whatever work was offered.

I had to adjust my budget. I owned two residences and sold one of them. I'd never done ads before, but Barry Levinson directed me in a coffee commercial. It traveled to Australia, where it repeated several times and generated a lot of money. During the filming of the advertisement, I learned that my accountant had been arrested and accused of conducting a Ponzi scheme. He received seven and a half years in prison. It made the news, but only briefly. It was a different age, and it did not garner the same kind of attention as the Bernie Madoff scandal, which occurred just a few years prior. I also attempted to keep it quiet. There is practically nothing worse for a celebrity than death, followed by bankruptcy.

My seminars were another huge discovery for me. In the past, I would frequently visit colleges and speak with the students there to get out there and perform for them. I'd tell them a bit about my life and let them ask questions. I'd bring books on stage by authors, playwrights, and poets I admired. I'd do some monologues and recite poems. That was something I really enjoyed doing. It was a connection with people I cared about. It felt good to share this stuff. It transported me back to the theatre. I did not get paid for it. I just did it.

Before I went bankrupt, I was doing films because I thought I could relate to the role and add something to it. Ocean's Thirteen turned out nicely. And I completed 88 minutes, which was a disaster. Then I did Righteous Kill with Bob De Niro, which was not terrific. But I did these things when I thought I had money, so it's not like I was doing them for money. I truly believed they could be good.

Jack and Jill was the first picture I produced after losing my money. To be honest, I did it because I had nothing else. Adam Sandler wanted me, and they paid me handsomely for it. So I went out and tried it, and it helped. Adam is a lovely person to work with and has become a close friend. He's also a great actor and a great person. An odd and dissonant combination of roles ensued. I liked The Humbling, a film I worked on with Barry Levinson. It was based on the work of Philip Roth, whom I met at a New York party. Roth was sitting in a chair, and he stared at me very seriously.

One of the benefits of working on Manglehorn was getting to know Harmony Korine, who performed a role in the film. Harmony was simply pure magic. He is the nephew of Joe Chaikin, who played the lead in the Living Theatre's performance of The Connection and founded the Open Theater, a wonderful experimental group in Manhattan that thrived in the 1960s and 1970s. I was a huge Joe admirer, and Harmony was captivating. We have a scene together that takes place in a setting that is a cross between a casino and a penny arcade. Harmony began improvising as his role in the film— he lasted ten minutes and was incredible. I was only playing my role, wondering where he would land. I felt like I was hearing James Joyce or Robin Williams. I couldn't believe what this man said. I know the material exists someplace, but it, like the original finale we shot, did not make it into the film.

I was doing these videos for nothing. Here I am, a person who has lost all of his money, working on films for nothing when I should be making money. However, they were not there for me at the moment. I always managed to receive offers. Some of these films were successful, while others failed. I had possibilities to work with good friends like Fisher Stevens, whom I had known for years. Fisher directed me in Stand Up Guys, and we had a good time together; it didn't exactly meet expectations, but it had potential. Then there was Danny Collins, which is one of my favorites and allowed me to work again with Christopher Plummer and other performers I've always liked, such as Annette Bening, Jennifer Garner, and my friend Bobby Cannavale. Dan Fogelman wrote Danny Collins with me. Danny is such a nice, talented guy. We all thought it stood a chance. I had a great time producing the film and still enjoy seeing it on TV. Many of the films I've worked on have a spark that we all hoped would catch fire. They may not have been as successful as some of my previous films, but I still like to acknowledge them because they have helped me over the years.

I felt I could still return to Broadway and hit the boards. Doing things this way also meant being away from Los Angeles and my children. But I couldn't do this kind of theater in Los Angeles, and I couldn't find this kind of money off Broadway, where I truly wanted to be. Oddly enough, when I needed money the most, I agreed to perform The Merchant of Venice onstage for free since it was Shakespeare in the Park, the brainchild of the great Joe Papp. I felt if we could make The Merchant of Venice work, it would be headed for Broadway. It turned out to be a relatively successful run, and I enjoyed being on stage in Central Park every night. I enjoyed doing it for free, for the people.

I adapted the Shylock character to suit what we were doing in the park. Daniel Sullivan was an excellent director who guided me through the rings. The old burning in the gut was back. Night after night, I'd walk up on stage and declare, "Tonight, I'll play this role, and I won't know what I'll do next." I will say my lines without knowing what the other actor will say next, and the words will come out naturally. I shall perform at the moment. I'll be alive and ready to participate in that type of setting. This was going to modify my deliveries and allow the nerves, body, and sinews to come alive—almost like improvisation, but with Shakespeare's wonderful lines.

A few years later, I was back on Broadway, this time in the stage production of Glengarry Glen Ross, and I knew I had failed. I was working with an excellent group of people, but I just did not have enough time to rehearse. In the film, I played Ricky Roma; onstage, I played Shelly Levene. Now I had to relearn everything. I'm not sure if I would have ever gotten to Shelly Levene—perhaps if I had persevered for twenty years. This was David Mamet dialogue, and sometimes I would get to a specific speech, not know the words, and make my own. The poor actors had to deal with me doing various things every night, but they were fantastic with me and always managed to stay on their feet. I'm still really close to a few of them; they're the type of friends you want to have. The audience seemed to enjoy it as well. The critics remain the critics.

You must understand that I would devour the content and work on it constantly to better understand my character. I was absorbing it for weeks of practice before presenting it each night. When I stepped onstage, it was all in me, but I threw it away and focused on the teleprompters. It was a little easier to just go for it. But it was difficult with China Doll on Broadway because people had written me off. When you become reputable, you are often viewed as a body of work rather than anything you accomplished last week. You are blessed with stuff you do not actually have. Your celebrity and acting abilities are overblown.

And sometimes movie stars do not return to the stage after a few failures since it is exhausting to perform live. And while you're dealing with all of this vitriol and resentment, you're performing onstage night after night. On China Doll, I was approaching eighty and dealing with all of it. I still have a part of me that feels this way, and I have to be aware of it at times. But I also know how rewarding it is to triumph in the face of a misjudgment—to say, "You're wrong about me, and I will survive," and that was a major drive for me to get there with China Doll. I am still standing here.

When I was fifteen, I played the lead role of producer Sidney Black in our school's production of the old Moss Hart play from the 1940s, Light Up the Sky, which Sam Levene made famous. I believe I was able to perform that role with a level of conviction that I have always strived for. I was on a tightrope, and I was a butterfly, flying up, up, and away to that place I call Nirvana. God offers it to you. God says you can go there. We're human. We are not on par with gods. We have all the other stuff hurled at us—all the cobwebs come our way. But when that is removed and you're flying, sweetheart, there's no feeling quite like it—at least none that I've had. So roughly half of my performances were successful, half were not so much, and others were in the toilet. But I am only human.

Chapter 13: The Undiscovered Country

It is time for my afternoon walk around the block. They claim it's healthy exercise, and I should be doing more of it at my age. So I put on my sunglasses and plugged in some earphones. I'm wearing a big old coat and I have white hair on my face. I'm wandering the streets like a polar bear, and the weather is becoming warmer. I'm an endangered species. I am at risk of extinction. Now I roam the streets, wondering if I'll have to face the brass to have a film done. I went there with Marty Bregman. He was a facilitator, hustler, and impresario. But I do not have him anymore. As the saying goes, our old pals are leaving one by one.

I am going to complete this film production on my own. I feel a fire inside myself because I know I've finally found something that works for me. And I feel like I've ruined my life by several decades. When you're a certain type of person, these things keep you going—passion projects practically keep us alive.

I have to say, I'm losing weight and feeling better. You'd think I was attractive or something to dress so horribly. I exacerbate it with the few looks I have left. A few years ago, I was on Broadway doing a show and was running late to the theater. Of course, those sons-of-bitches took a photo of me with a hood on at the stage door. I wasn't even on the curb; I was still in the gutter. I'm bending over and looking up at them, just like any bagman you've seen on the street. I'm carrying two tiny shopping bags, and I can't recall what's inside them. People are undoubtedly thinking, "This fucking guy is a miser." Is that what he's developing into? He has money in those bags. He cashes the checks and puts money in the bags. This is Broadway's highest paid dramatic performer. And does he look like that? Equity is going to kick me out of the union.

I've done some television and had some excellent experiences. I played Roy Cohn in Angels in America, a film written and directed by Tony Kushner and Mike Nichols, two of the best directors I've ever worked with. I did Hunters for David Weil. For David Mamet, I played Phil Spector, while for Barry Levinson, I played Jack Kevorkian and Joe Paterno. They were all excellent parts. I received appreciation and recognition for such performances. I even won a few Emmys. It was an incredible experience for me to meet Jack Kevorkian in preparation for his role. I spent time with him in Detroit, and he was among the top three smartest individuals I'd ever met. He was simply the most pro-life person I had ever met—someone who, on the actual battlefield of war, would transfuse the blood of dead troops in the hopes of saving the living. He even tested this experiment on himself, contracting hepatitis in the process. He believed in his actions. Jack was a true zealot, the type that goes right out the window—that's what he did, and it landed him in prison for eight years.

Eleonora Duse, the great star of the nineteenth century and regarded the best actress, along with Sarah Bernhardt, played Juliet on stage at the age of sixty—and Juliet is meant to be thirteen. Ian McKellen, a wonderful actor, is playing Hamlet on screen in his nineties, which I applaud. Most people recommend that you play Hamlet when you've lived longer, and I believe Ian will be particularly sensitive to the play's wisdom. I believe in his efforts and eagerly await their results. Unfortunately, one must accommodate oneself.

I've always wanted to play Napoleon. There was also a moment when Stanley Kubrick was interested in working with me, but it never materialized. Then I finally obtained a script that worked from William Mastrosimone. His story took place in Napoleon's latter years, after he was banished and lost all power, but I was too old to play the role. That specific Napoleon was a role I knew I could play—it's rare to come across a fictional figure with whom you can identify and comprehend as much as I did with Mastrosimone's book. It's a fantastic job, but all of the streaming services rejected it, claiming that the writing was too advanced, despite the fact that I knew my age. It's terrible that I wasn't able to play it, but it's so excellent that hopefully someone lucky will get the opportunity.

I had no idea what those things meant until I performed in a play or read about them in a novel. It was in The Brothers Karamazov, I believe I read it there. Otherwise, I went through life without thinking about such things. I had no idea that if someone died, you received something. How do you live without that concept in your mind? That lifestyle has a certain purity. Death does not guarantee that you will receive anything. Death just implies that you will lose someone, and how you feel is determined by who died. Some are a grain of salt, while others make you feel like you've lost a part of your organs.

Fame alters your life; an avalanche of stimuli begins to bombard you. There's some good, some bad, and some ugly, and most people find it difficult to deal with. It's why so many people turn to drugs and alcohol to protect themselves from what life throws at them, especially when they're young and inexperienced. Most people lack the thick skin necessary to endure all the lies and assumptions made about them. Fame brings money, and money brings lawsuits; nevertheless, money also brings access to top doctors, which is useful if you want to live. I know wealthy folks whose closest friends are doctors. They make sure to become best friends with doctors.

I realized in my late sixties that one must take care of oneself. I had surgery on my neck's carotid arteries, and the surgeon hit a nerve, causing me to lose use of one of my vocal cords. The artery was cleaned, but the vocal chord remained paralyzed for approximately a year. When you're an actor who relies heavily on your voice, you want to prevent this. The live theater was out. You need a projection. Without a voice cord, I was stuck. I didn't think using my paralyzed vocal cord would help me get well. I do not have that level of medical expertise. However, I have an urge to perform. I was getting ready to recite Marc Antony's funeral oration from Julius Caesar as part of one of my lectures. I was working with a classical composer who scored the scene, and a sound engineer who added some effects that made us feel like we were part of a mob gathered in ancient Rome in 44 BC. Every time I concluded that speech, I lost my voice for nearly five hours, but I still attempted. Sure, my cracked voice wasn't what audiences were used to, and I don't think my delivery ever went where I intended it to, but it had returned. I believe it has something to do with my brain or my prayers to God.

My death was unexpectedly reported on YouTube, which was a horrific sensation. On the other hand, I actually died once. It happened to me at the beginning of the epidemic, when I had my first round of COVID. I was experiencing high fevers and becoming dehydrated, so I had a nurse come to my house and insert an IV to give me fluids. The man who was administering the needles and running the IV bag was quite friendly. I thought, "Jeez, I like this guy." It would be great if I could recall his name.

Then I opened my eyes to see six paramedics and two physicians in my living room, clothed in protective garments that made them appear to be from outer space. There was an ambulance outside my door. My assistant, Michael, had contacted 911 when the guy who was assisting with the IV informed him that I didn't have a pulse. I was given monoclonal antibodies, steroids, and everything else at home because I had no intention of going to a hospital. I made it through, and within a few days, I was back up and running. But I feel I died that day.

Amerigo Tot, who played my bodyguard in The Godfather: Part II, was an amazing artist and sculptor who knew Picasso. He informed me that when he went to visit Picasso, he extended his hand, and Picasso shook it limply. He gets to the canvas—whoosh. He expends it. Amerigo told me this story, and I understood some of it. But, who can relate? Not at the age I was then. In a strange way, I'm more renowned now than I ever was—not because of the work I do, but because of my relationships with other individuals, appearances in certain things, and living in Hollywood. I got lucky. I appeared in three films in a row that each had a significant influence, beginning with Once Upon a Time in Hollywood. I didn't get paid a lot for it, but I was working with Quentin Tarantino, Leo DiCaprio, Brad Pitt, and Margot Robbie, and I enjoyed the role. Leo presented a fantastic monologue in which he said everything there was to say about this sector in 1969. However, films have their own rhythms, and Tarantino's scene ended up lasting about two minutes. I don't fault him for it. He had cause to do so.

I think Once Upon a Time in Hollywood is an excellent picture. And just being there gave me cachet. Then comes The Irishman. Years ago, Bob De Niro and Martin Scorsese approached me and discussed what they planned to do. I was all for it. And now, there's a script. I go out and do it. I have a significant role. I'm nominated for an Oscar, up against Brad Pitt, Joe Pesci, Anthony Hopkins, and Tom Hanks. That night, I had no issue embracing my status as a loser among those guys.

However, I found myself back in that setting. I was visible. Next thing you know, I'm in House of Gucci, a hot film starring Adam Driver, Lady Gaga, Jared Leto, and my good pal Jeremy Irons. It did not receive the same reaction as the others, but it performed well at the box office. Plus, it was directed by one of the all-time greats, Ridley Scott, whom I adored as someone so talented and enjoyable to work for.

I am an actor. It's what I do, and every now and then, I'm fortunate enough to find roles that allow me to express myself, do a decent job, and feel as if I made something. There is still room for that. That boy I was, that little fourteen-year-old kid at the High School of Performing Arts who broke through that door in the play Light Up the Sky, that was an absolutely living, breathing thing that I did, and

I did it with no idea what I was doing, not even knowing that it was a form of expression, and it was wonderful. And reading Strindberg's Creditors helped me understand my relationship with the world. Acting allowed me to expand my reach into new domains. This discovery—and it was a discovery—goes a little deeper than I can describe. I'm trying to be as near to it as possible, because it altered my life. This is how profound it was. I had an insight. It did not imply that I was a brilliant actor or anything. I just assumed that this was what would keep me alive.

You may receive a lot of money now for teaching these master workshops about acting on the internet. I never went near it because I don't know what I can say to any actor who may be of assistance—because, like so many things in life, it's so personal. If necessary, I would advise you to repeat it until it becomes ingrained in you. I hope it does, but to be honest, most of the time it won't. I'd also add that it may sound simple, but it's true: believe in the tale you're presenting as if it were genuine. Finally, I can identify the message on Charles Bukowski's gravestone: "Do not try." I guess I understand what he means.

Chapter 14: Who Speaks of Triumph? To Endure Is Everything

In the 1990s, I was a guest at a major event, an awards ceremony for the Directors Guild, and I was asked to give a speech on Francis Ford Coppola. We were in the midst of this grand hall, with its high ceilings and high-class décor, when I noticed another man my age working as a busboy or waiter. He was pulling a cart loaded with plates and wearing a uniform, a sort of small tuxedo that was required for the job. I had no idea what his title was, but I knew his name: Marty-P, an old friend from the South Bronx. And the moment I saw his face, all I could think about was the last time I saw him. Marty-P and I had been standing with the rest of the gang on a store rooftop. These rooftops were significantly lower to the ground than the tenements, allowing for easy access. We enjoyed our freedom there and hung out like birds, smoking and drinking. However, Cliffy had just thrown a water balloon the size of a potato sack. It slammed into the bonnet of a passing police car—pow!—and we had to hurriedly jump from the roof to avoid the policemen. Marty-P appeared to be struggling to make the leap, and I was shouting at him to do it, which he eventually did. We were gone as soon as we escaped to the nearest alleyway; they would never find us.

At a certain age, you develop a peculiar sensation in which your memories flash before your eyes without your permission. I was recently tempted to return to my old neighborhood, but I realized there was nothing that resembled what I grew up in. The world I am describing will not happen again. These stories are all that remain from that time, location, and mindset. Perhaps that's why I wrote this book. I want to go home. These recollections keep transporting me back to a location I enjoyed being. When I reflect on my life, I realize how fortunate I was. There was satisfaction in that life. There was hope in that life. In my thoughts, I return to the Bronx streets of my youth, looking at the stores and people. I see the lads I grew up with climbing on top of the massive girders that span the front of the 174th Street Bridge, overlooking a stretch of the Bronx River. There we were, our legs dangling off the girders above the bridge's entrance, as the drivers passed underneath, staring up at us and figuring that these boys were insane. You have to understand how risky that was. My mother took me to the same bridge when I had a whooping cough. She was advised I needed to get near the water. I believe they meant the ocean, but we just had the Bronx River.

It was as if he had transformed into Pat O'Brien from a 1930s film, the monotonous old street priest who warns James Cagney to straighten up and fly right or he will be executed. All I wanted to do was push an apple into his mouth and get back to dividing the lettuce and cucumbers. He was a working guy, which was OK, and he had good intentions, but he was now instructing me how to live, and I am twelve and a half years old. I am simply trying to get through the day. I'm not going to die with a piece of decaying fruit in my hand while you preach about how wonderful life can be if I simply do what you say. Fuck you and the pineapple container you arrived on, friend. Of course, I didn't say it out loud; I simply gave him the A-OK nod, as most kids do, but I did think it, and then I quit and went back out there with my mongrel pals.

When you're young, you don't remember much—you talk about yesterday or the day before. You are building them as you live. I have many memories, and I don't need historic structures or physical items to reconnect with them. Sometimes it's a sight, sound, or scent; other times, it's just a sensation. I'll just feel cold, and all of a sudden, I'm nineteen or twenty years old again, shivering and shaking in a Manhattan boarding house on Tenth Avenue, after wandering alone in the frigid snow. My room was a few floors up and tiny, but it had a window through which I could see people on Tenth Avenue coming and going in the snow, and that small window with its view made it appealing. But the coat I was wearing was soaked from head to toe. Like all my outfits, I got it at a thrift store for a few dollars. I couldn't have been more wet or fatigued, and my second-hand clothing was leaking and coming apart. My room's steam radiator had gone berserk, spraying the bed in moisture and leaving me without heat.

The next morning, I awoke feeling alive but dizzy. I was chilly and shaking uncontrollably. I realized I had a temperature. I knew I had to go to the hospital. I made it to Bellevue's emergency ward and waited in their clinic for hours, a twenty-year-old wreck.

I did not, however, visit the outpatient clinic, but rather my cousin Mark's flat on Arlington Avenue in the West Bronx, beneath the El. My cousin Mark and the lady he was living with took care of me, putting me on a couch while I nursed a 104-degree fever. I was there for days to heal. I'm not sure why I didn't visit my grandmother. I suppose I went to Mark's because he lived closer to Manhattan. I adore my cousin like a brother.

It seemed like I was always in need of someone to care for me. Many years later, while I was performing David Mamet's American Buffalo on the East Coast, the renowned film star Elizabeth Taylor was also performing on Broadway, and I quickly became acquainted with her. We would hang around and enjoy one other's company. She was a wonderful actor with a kind heart, and she met some of the people in my life, including Jim Bulleit and Jimmy Hayden. We would discuss everything. I'd always ask her about Richard Burton, whom she'd been married to twice and who, along with Marlon, was my favorite actor; she'd sometimes humor me, sometimes dismiss me. She was both a normal person and a walking, talking treasure.

I paid her a visit in the early 2000s at her stunningly magnificent home in Los Angeles. As I gazed at the walls, which were adorned with paintings by Renoir, Matisse, and Picasso, I thought, "What a place to live." Imagine waking up every day and feeling inspired. When she was in New York, she would come to my country house, and I would prepare her spaghetti. It amazes me that these things actually happened to me, and I can't even verify it anymore. 34th Street East, the movie theater where I worked as an usher and watched the classic The Red Shoes perhaps a hundred times, is no longer there. I felt like a shadow in the theater, and I liked it. They put that monkey suit on me, which I didn't enjoy, but I stood there in the dark, staring at the screen. The Rugoff theaters were transforming movies into cinema, appealing to a more affluent audience. They typically hired men as ushers and women as cashiers. The only condition for being employed as an usher was that you be pretty attractive. If you were someone who was in and out of it, like I was, you simply did what they instructed you to do. I could use the flashlight while standing in one location. It sounds simple enough, but I would still get fired from these places on a regular basis.

Outside of these occupations, I continued to attempt to act and audition for roles. Charlie accompanied me once to the Hudson Playhouse in Greenwich Village, where I had been called back for not one, but two plays. I'd already gone to read for them, and both directors loved me the first time, so I assumed I'd get one of the roles. There was some hope. But I didn't receive either, which is a common experience for performers.

While working as an usher, I took it upon myself to refer acquaintances for jobs. I even secured Charlie a job as an usher at Carnegie Hall of all things. We'd arrived. Okay, I was still just an usher, but this was Carnegie Hall. I recall having a tremendous crush on a pretty lesbian girl who worked there. I'm not sure what happened to her, but I genuinely liked her, even if she didn't appear interested in me. So here's Charlie in a tuxedo, looking like a master of ceremonies; he could be a maître d' at a restaurant or handing out Oscars at the big ceremony.

I was gone, pounding the streets in search of another usher job. By that point, I knew what I wanted to be: an usher—no, an actress. You'd think I'd be down in the dumps after being fired so frequently. Or that I might be nervous, wondering where I'd find the next job. But I was always confident that one would come along—the jobs were only a means to an end, and they would continue to come as long as I pursued my calling. And New York City gave me many resources to pursue my passion. I don't have any recollections like that today. I don't remember things as vividly as I used to, and this isn't due to dementia. Yes, I am still alive, but in a much more predictable environment. Thank God for my children—as you can tell, I adore them and am delighted they have their own lives. Actors have their own lives. That is why, for me, labor has always represented life—something that opens the door and allows the spirit to emerge.

I just saw him the other day and he is four months old. This little infant is now talking and really getting into it. I couldn't believe how much he was saying. Not saying anything, just infant gibberish, but speaking as if he really wanted to say anything. I assumed he was attempting to contact me. He's chatting to me and telling me where he's from. He's trying to make me feel better, and I'd like to thank him for reassuring me that everything will be fine. Thank you, youngster.

I'm not sure how much my youngster will understand. When I try to explain what it was like to grow up in the South Bronx to young people, I feel like I'm explaining Oliver Twist's London, Thornton Wilder's Grover's Corners, or the small town in Texas from The Last Picture Show. And I'm not talking about the Bronx, let alone New York City; it's a small, provincial world with its own little community. I had no idea what was going on a few streets away, on Vyse Avenue or Longfellow. What I knew was our block.

An entire cosmos existed beneath the El on the White Plains Road line, just a short walk from my place. There was the barbershop where my grandfather used to take me when I was a tiny boy to get my hair trimmed, and I had to sit on a box in the barber's chair because I was too small. Looking above and to the left from my chair, I could see the El flying by, transporting people to and from our small neighborhood. Just across the street, under that El, was a small café where my mother would take me to the movies when I was four or five years old in the early 1940s. I can still remember the warmth of that luncheonette, with its blue-and-white checkerboard-tiled walls, the melancholy songs from wartime emanating from the radio, and the pretty girl working the counter, the one with the white ribbon in her blond hair and the blue bow on her apron, smiling at me. Just a few doors down was the Dover Theatre on Boston Road, where my mother and I would see movies. My mother was everything to me. She had a knack for detecting impending events.

My pals and I had the entire world to ourselves, as far as we knew. We didn't receive sex education in school; we learned it on the streets through hearsay. Life was ours. Let us do something! Let's go somewhere. Let's take the train downtown or stroll and strut. Just keep clear from the exhibit cases Cliffy seems to be drawn to. We couldn't play stickball in the late spring or summer since the sun had set. That was when it was time to seek out some turmoil, some adventure. Maybe there'd be a Boy Scout meeting at one of the junior high schools that we could disrupt, shake things up, and get chased around the hallways by the custodians. We'd zip around and duck into the shadowy classrooms, looking for somewhere to hide. These institutions were massive, two or three stories tall, with classrooms everywhere, and they seemed luxury to us.

There I am with my pals in the abandoned lots around 174th Street, where we would always end up at the end of the day, waiting for the half mass of light to fade into darkness. We're playing around, wondering what's going on and what will happen next. My pals ask

144

me to accompany them elsewhere. But not for me, not tonight. Cliffy, Bruce, and Petey were ready to go, along with a few other guys, when my mother called. Our windows did not face the street, so I could hear my mother from the roof of our building.

By the time dad died, I had already achieved success as an actor. I learned about Bruce's funeral while I was at work, so I went to his burial in a barren cemetery in the Bronx. I got there on a cold, cloudy day in January. Bruce's mother and another woman, presumably her friend or Bruce's aunt, stood alone on a hill, no one else in sight for miles, peering down at Bruce's body in a box. I dashed up to his mother, whom I recognized from a long time ago, when she would carry young Bruce his small jug of chocolate milk in front of us all, right there on the street.

But the elder woman beside his mother—she could have been an aunt or cousin—spoke eloquently about Bruce at his graveside. What she said was not generic rhetoric; it was observant, and it was so accurate that it surprised me. Bruce was someone I grew up with, who would defend me if somebody attempted to be a tough man with me, and whom I directed in the comedic revues we staged in Greenwich Village café theaters in the 1960s. What this woman had to say about him was blatantly true. Only someone who was intelligent and mature enough to grasp life and a guy like Bruce could articulate it. I thought I knew him, but with just a few phrases, she proved that I didn't, not on that level. I shuddered at the depths of its understanding. I was in awe of it.